# LUMINOUS

# JOURNEYS

*Natural Portals*
*to the Spirit World*

*Pathways*  SUPPORT.
INFORMATION.
EDUCATION.
NOW.

breast and gynecological cancer
support groups and programs

The Connection
for Women and Families

79 Maple Street • Summit, NJ 07901
908.273.4242

www.theconnectiononline.org

ES

# LUMINOUS
# JOURNEYS

*Natural Portals
to the Spirit World*

## Sharon Blessum

To order additional copies of this book, contact:
Xlibris Corporation
1-888-795-4274
www.Xlibris.com
Orders@Xlibris.com

*This book is lovingly dedicated*
*to my parents*
*in gratitude*
*for the gift of life*
*for early lessons of honoring nature*
*for reverencing*
*the created world*
*and the Creative Source:*


*Kermit Reuben Blessum*
*Fern Rohrer Blessum*


*and to my ancestors*
*who tilled the soil*
*knew God and Nature*
*and prayed for me*

# *Acknowledgments*

The companions of life feed our souls, keep our bodies whole. I am indebted to the many forms in which Spirit has appeared to me in a simple, loving comrade: My sweet cat, Mela, chants to me in purrs. My sons and sisters, father and mother (in spirit), daughters-in-law, granddaughters, and sisters' families, hold me in a circle of loving attachments. Spirit guides uphold me daily. Rocks, trees, clouds, snow, stars, fields, flowers, mountains, meadows, and animals offer living connection.

Though many dear ones remain unnamed here, particular friends have been heartlines during the writing of this book. Cathy Higgins, Julie Jaarsma-Holdom, Nancy Hubley, Sylvia Pearl, Anne Burton, Vicki Christianson, Helen Lindsey, Mark Ettin, and Lona Fowler help me keep body and soul together. Joan Weimer spent many hours with earlier writings, generously teaching me with her astute observations. Nancy Hubley edited this manuscript with heart and skill. Jeanette Gagan lovingly encouraged and guided me through the steps toward publishing. Meinrad Craighead gave the hospitality of her immeasurable wisdom and creative encouragement. Leigh Rosoff gave heart and soul, eye and instinct to a creative collaboration, which helped me through several drafts. I am indebted to her. And then there are my psychotherapy clients and the women of the Healing Path Circle that meet with me each week for drumming and spiritual practice. And those who gave me permission to use their experiences, however disguised and edited, for this book. How rich I am to know these dear human beings. I salute them all for their courage, compassion, and capacity to grow.

Under, around, and through it all, is simply Spirit.

My Beloved among beloveds.

# CONTENTS

Invitation

s

You

are invited

to journey

through natural portals

to a Luminous Landscape

I'm looking out the window at the large evergreen dripping with fresh rain. My eyes take in the liquid green, then . . . then . . . well, where did I go? Suddenly I'm back. Perhaps you like to spend time-out-of time like I do.

These pages invite you to sacred time—bid you to pass through openings in nature, to another world, to let your ordinary consciousness give way to something deeper. You are summoned to intuition's wisdom. You are encouraged to listen for the voice within. You are called to the sacred landscape.

Spiritual power/presence is like electricity in a room waiting to be turned on. We simply need to connect to that power. We are meant to live connected. Journeys through natural portals bring access to that power, that place of luminosity. Your human life can be transformed back to its original stellar quality. We come from the stars and return to them. And on the way, we have great help.

stardust/earthdust

one creation

all is one

one

O

O me

O you

O us

O wondrous beings

from the godheart

mother womb

spewed into being

popping up on the earthplane

looking around in slight disorientation

how to manage this

how to survive it

how to find our place

how to connect with others

how to help

how to serve

how to get well

how to fix

how to thrive

O Spirit, come in,

help us see that we lostalittlebit in our birthmoment

but that godness from which we were born

that spirit world of our eternal home

was not left behind but is here

needs us to learn anew

how to connect.

May our eyes open

hearts open

beings open

that we might see again

the invisible ones

SHARON BLESSUM

who gather about us
who come and go from their daily rounds
to ours
may thy great will inform our own;
for You lead us to joy and wellbeing,
our own
and the planet's.

I recently had a little group here at my Farm for a day of sacred play. We drummed and danced, journeyed into the sacred landscape together, made "soup of abundance," did photo art, and gathered around the hearth to read poems, sing songs, and tell of our personal moments when the ordinary breaks through to the extraordinary.

I seem to live on that bridge, so the "extraordinary" is very close for me. Yet life being what it is, I still need to set aside particular times with a clear intention to live in my soul's connection to Spirit. As you probably know, intention is the most important aspect of the spiritual life. Where our intention is, there will we live.

I went on a three-day retreat over New Year's here at the Farm. I knew I'd be guided by Spirit; I didn't know the full moon would wake me at three A.M. to initiate the experience! During the night, the moon called me to the windowseat in my room where I look out into the trees dancing in the moonlight. Branches blow wildly and two limbs outside the window form a springboard for me to leap from one consciousness to another. Moving portals, small, ever-changing, seem dangerous because they open and close like scissors. Yet, I know just on the other side is safety and an adventure.

I leap through the shifting openings and am taken to heights new to me. In ordinary consciousness, the speed of time is torturous to me these days. We are all hyperstimulated by our society. But our spiritual sentience is bombarded also at times, moving at a fast clip. An acceleration of lessons and new ways comes and I know to pay attention. The Great Shaman has hold of me and offers yet another initiation into higher consciousness.

In the night
I sit in the north window
bare branches near enough to touch
separated by a pane tell me there will not be pain
though tomorrow I must be dismembered
for initiation into this new year
O
a full moon
shines in the western sky
an early morning
OH
I who never see dawn watch the light open on the farm
branches and blades of grass yawn and stretch
toward the new year of night and day, outside and inside,
matter and spirit
the tree limbs move faster
my own momentum won't let me sleep
we sense something coming
in this middle world between two realms
we perk up together
the year begins
not in stillness but in a calling
come come come
something is coming
I better get some rest
OH

Many hours later, I'm still looking out the windows in the middle of the night. The trees are still, no branches move. The limbs I stood on have disappeared. And so the retreat begins. I am willing, but wish I could pin life down just for a moment. It is a time of great changes. Nothing pauses. When I finally sleep, I am taken into a dark room of mystery. Even in my sleep, teachers are busy with me. When these days ended, I was cleared and empowered.

A few weeks after my retreat, I heard of a woman who retreated at home for a month. She paid her bills, cleaned her house, told family and friends not to call, and began thirty days in the wilderness/wonderfulness of her solitude. She went to work each day but went straight home to write, pray, paint, whatever Spirit prompted her to do.

Self-designed retreats with clear intentions cost no money and offer tremendous rewards. Mary pondered. Jesus went off into the hills to pray. Alone time is key to staying on your healing path. And just think, you're with your best friend!

Trees, rocks, sky, water, caves, creatures, flowers and all forms of nature provide portals, thresholds that invite us from here to there. I get pulled into prairies, lifted onto clouds, stopped in my tracks by a rock with coded messages. You know the feeling. Time and space are altered as we slip into another state of mind. We step through openings into the spirit world. You are invited to thrill in the ordinary for it is a doorway to the extraordinary.

The journey begins at a threshold. Maybe you will be invited to sit under a tree or on a bench near the ocean or at the top of a mountain or in the woods near a stream. Maybe Spirit will first tug at you when you are jogging through a park, riding an ocean wave, or gazing at the night sky. Open your heart and eyes, give yourself permission to say yes to the invitation, to pass through a natural portal from this world to the other. I would gladly meet you to cheer you on. We need community for support and holding as we live our challenging lives. Those of us who sit in circle together or walk a similar path draw on our common energyfield for the living of our days. We have sacred connection. We are not alone. If we meet at the same place each time, our energy grows there and the air holds our names. We come closer, from what appears to be our separate selves. Remember Antoine De Saint Exupery's words in "The Little Prince":

> "You must be very patient," replied the fox. "First, you will
> sit down at a little distance from me—like that—in the
> grass. I shall look at you out of the corner of my eye, and you

will say nothing. Words are the source of misunderstanding. But you will sit a little closer to me every day . . . ."

The next day the little prince came back.

Spirit will keep appointment with us also. "Where two or three are gathered . . . ."

The spirit world exists parallel to our ordinary world, a place as real and knowable as this one is seeable and smellable. This spirit realm, from which we came and to which we go, is inhabited by angels, ancestors, animal guides, spirit teachers. They seem to live in a grand choreography which includes interaction with us. They watch and wait for us to leap through the doorway towards them. "Behold, I stand at the door and knock." We will know them fully when we leave this earth, but we can visit them now. The worlds meet at luminous intersections. The shaman knows it. Jesus knew it. We can know it. He came to show us the Way. He knew the Light. As have others.

My heart and vision opened to the spirit world through drumming and chanting, calling me out of life-as-usual. Drumming is an ancient aid to move us into an altered state of consciousness in which we are less in our five senses and more able to experience other dimensions of reality. My path is shamanism. But there are other ways of access too. Maybe you use reiki, ritual, mantra, or music, or meditation. Maybe you sit in silence by the water, on the bridge where the two worlds meet. Maybe you will light a candle and incense. Sing an old hymn. Or drum and chant. Maybe some deep breathing. Or tibetan bells. You will find your way to move from the edge of consciousness into an altered state where illumination awaits you. The maps are many, the territory one. Won.

Won only as we learn to walk through the looking glass, find the extra door in the wardrobe, fall down the hole with Alice. Remember when we were little how we seemed to know things that no one else was talking about? Maybe you remember the enchantment of a secret garden or an unseen friend. Babies seem to smile and laugh at beings they see that we cannot. The young

SHARON BLESSUM

tell us about their invisible companions and the dying tell about the loved ones who gather to help them pass over. Other cultures encourage this capacity; ours does not. But we need not be exempt from knowing the spirit world. We just need access through opening our hearts and vision.

Fasten your spiritual seat belt—not because you are traveling fast, but because you are heading into uncharted waters. You are adventuring into unfamiliar territory. This spiritual territory will be the foundation for the healing of wounds and the ecstasies of Spirit.

Maybe this is a good time to mention that seven-letter word, "skeptic." It's kind of a dirty word in our spiritual work. But that little voice exists in all of us and we probably do ourselves a favor to pause and acknowledge it so it doesn't start getting loud and dissuading us from our adventures. I certainly started this process with skepticism!

I was at lunch with friends when someone mentioned journeying into the spirit world. I wasn't interested. She said that on her first journey she was turned into a bug. I didn't want to be a bug!

Well, my first journey was like the proverbial fish to water and access to the spirit world became as natural to me as breathing.

Doubt gave way to certainty as my innards changed, my life was transformed and I truly was not the person I used to be. Or WAS I the person I used to be, long before I could remember?

When I'm teaching introductory workshops to this path, someone always articulates the sense that they are making this up, that these images are only their imagination. We discredit our imagination, forgetting it is the great tool of artists, writers, scientists, any who use vision to fantasize beyond the tried and true. Imagination is a wondrous part of our humanness and can be very helpful as we begin spiritual trance work. The people who are highly left-brain often have underdeveloped imagination and they struggle to let go of mindchatter. They often envy the more intuitive people in a workshop. If imagination helps you begin, be grateful.

You will sense when imagination has given way and Spirit has given over. You will begin to have experiences that you wouldn't know how to imagine. Surrender your wonderful intelligence to another part of yourself and you will find heightening capacity to interact with the spirit world.

Many people say that quantum physicists are among the most spiritual people in our society. I wouldn't doubt that. You probably know that scientific studies have been studying energy, and have proven the power of prayer by measuring results of people prayed for versus people not prayed for. Scientists have identified parts of the brain that change as we experience spirits, visions, the oneness of creation. I have NO question; I have NO skepticism, about what the power of spiritual energy and experience of Spirit has done in my life. My life experiences have made me a believer in the spirit world. However, if it turned out that we humans were producing the whole spiritual experience through our brains and that none of it existed outside our belief, it wouldn't matter. It would still be the reality that heals and transforms us. Our language is all we have to communicate what we experience. I'm glad we have it! But, it may force us to label and categorize things that aren't really that way. If God is external or internal or both, It can still transform lives as the EnergySource effects energy fields. If I experience the world as fearful and come to believe in a demonic presence that permeates people and makes them dangerous to me, I will create a reality accordingly and may become pathologically paranoid or go out to murder all those dangerous people out there—all because of a reality I created. I made it true and changed the world because of it. So, we could do the same in an opposite direction. Spiritual experiences unlock a profoundly loving heart and definitely bring change into the world. So IF, that were only a reality we created, it would still be the best thing we are capable of. So, the whole issue of skepticism is irrelevant to me. Journeys to the spirit world heal me and bring only good to my relationships with all created beings. If I die and there is no more, I will have served the world in a far more loving way because of the joys that I experienced in the spirit realm. And if I don't venture into this dimension, I will have missed a profound aspect of the human experience.

My healing and teaching work with others has only confirmed my belief in Spirit and the powerful presence of spirit beings. Yet, I have occasionally worked with people who seem to manifest so little change that I become disheartened. Early in this work, when discouraged about a person who'd been in therapy with me for a long time, I decided to journey about my doubts.

> I am taken to a teacher whose very composure is gentle with me. I speak to her, "I must confess that I feel some skepticism today. How has this world become so real and important to me? I don't want to doubt it, because it is the source of my healing and knowledge. But you can understand how new and mysterious it is to me. In my ordinary world there is so much stress, especially with this woman who is so angry with me about her depressive ways."

> She responds, "Yes, of course I understand. This is not an experience you ever learned about from anyone else, though you will be starting to read books of people who do shamanic healing. You are very alone in your ways because Spirit has taught you in the privacy of your own home. You were not one of those adopted by a native tribe!"

> She goes on, "Your task is to trust. Remember how you had to learn trust when you first started journeying to the spirit world and finding healing for yourself. You learned there is a whole realm working to meet your needs."

> "Yes, I felt my needs had never been met before."

> "Sharon, that is not quite true. As you look back over your life you will see that your needs were always met. Not in the way that you wished in ordinary reality, perhaps, but we were there

and you were helped along in your own growth and evolution.
Now you are conscious of Spirit's work with you."

"I have learned that the spirits have more good intended for
me than I would know how to imagine!"

Now I start smiling because the journey that was triggered by
my lack of faith for someone else's healing has been redirected to a
reminder of the wondrous work on my behalf. I'm filled with joy
and appreciation at this world of helpers that I now know.

Sometimes in our drumming circle, we hear singing or other
drumming that is not coming from us. We sense the presence of
those from the other side, an eternal drumming circle which gathers
invisibly around us. Maybe you have sensed us drumming softly
for you, as you may have sensed monastics praying for you and the
world. Maybe you have long felt a call to return to your own spiritual
life or discover a path that feels helpful to your soul. In the next
chapter of *Luminous Journeys*, you will begin learning a spiritual
process to aid your access to the spirit world. You will have
opportunity to record your experiences in this journal. You will be
guided past your five senses to that intuitive part of you that has
always known there is more than meets the eye! Or ear!

You will have your own way of using this journal, *Luminous
Journeys*. Whether you use it in the morning or evening, on a daily
basis, once a week, set aside a monthly retreat for yourself, or meet
regularly with friends to share these pages, let your heart guide
you to a sacred ritual for yourself. Surround yourself with objects
sacred to you, and let these pages be a launching pad for your
travels into the land of healing and guidance.

Remember the old hymn, "Balm in Gilead"?
There is a balm in Gilead
To make the wounded whole
There is a balm in Gilead
To heal the sin-sick soul

Healing balm is the essence we seek. Where is Gilead? In the next chapters you will learn how to go there. You will find openings in nature that welcome you to sanctuaried space where you will do this work. You will pass through portals to a place set apart from the usual cares of your world. You will learn access to the realms of Spirit. Balm in Gilead.

Log on, human beings.
Use the password given you at the start of creation.
Access spiritspace, past cyberspace.
Move from internet to innernet
where abundant resource awaits you.
Link up to the intricate and elegant web.
Be online with infinite possibilities.
Boot up your system.
Sacred technology will transform your world.

Intentions focus spiritual energy. These chapters, our sessions together, will suggest intentions to help you evolve on this path. At times, you may feel a need to modify that intention to be more specific about an issue for which you need healing or guidance. Perhaps you need help with a relationship, an issue at work, a life change. Invoke the presence of Spirit, let yourself be guided as if by a Mother whose very presence means safety and security. Nothing harmful will happen; you always have free choice available.

When you journey into the spirit world, you move from your spirit home through a natural portal into the realm of teachers and guides. As this process of entering the spirit world becomes familiar and comfortable to you, you will need to clearly state intentions for your visit to the spirit world. As you sow, you reap. As you journey with clarity of intention, you will receive clear benefits. For example, if I say I am journeying with my power animal to get guidance for my life, I might go off in many different unfocused directions with a mishmash of scenes. The experiences might all be relevant in some way, but not specifically helpful. If I begin with the statement that I am journeying with my power animal to receive guidance on a particular aspect of a relationship between me and a work colleague, I will receive specific help on that issue. My intention is the key.

We walk in the direction in which we look. We form from the vision that we hold. We become what we cherish. Watch where you fasten your energy for it is there that you will grow. Claiming the intention of the moment and of your life is the key to soulmaking. Your spiritual path can only manifest the level of your intention.

Perhaps you are conflicted about many things. You say one thing and mean another. At the level of soul this will not work. It is with integrity that we work with intentions; it is with consciousness that we choose where we will put our energy.

An intention is not the same as an affirmation, though an affirmation can grow out of an intention. In my experience, affirmations only work when they come out of your own soul's truth. You cannot live off someone else's affirmation or truth. Nor can you successfully live out of an intention someone else has for you.

Let your journeys follow paths to fields of joy. Spiritual beings, adventures, healings and teachings await you. Maybe you will pass through tunnels and radiant colors; maybe you will see nothing; maybe you discover blessings stored up for you since the beginning of time. You may not remember this familiar place, but you will know it as your homeland, from which you want to live. Rather than being lured away from the world to here, you can make this your center and travel out into the world from here. As is commonly said, we are not human beings having a spiritual experience, we are spiritual beings having a human experience.

When you are forming your intentions and becoming more adept at your spiritual work, let that little skeptical self be taken into the spirit world. You'll find humor and compassion. In our humanness we entertain many traits, but gradually the validity of our experience takes over our inner house and the skeptic no longer has a landlord offering space. "Sorry, you can't live here anymore," we say to that diminishing voice within us.

Which reminds me that hospitality is an intention worth cultivating on our healing path. Too often we have given space to anyone who wants to occupy our energy field. Out of our lack of self-worth and not valuing our soul's wellbeing, we let ourselves be intruded on, manipulated, used for purposes not always for our highest good. As we learn more about spiritual energy and the power of our intentions, we will want to keep a clean house within because we learn how our very health suffers if we are hospitable to toxic energy.

As we become clear and conscious about what energy we do not want to entertain, because it is not healthy for us, we then are free to choose the people, places, and animals that are nourishing to our soul. And when we are willing to serve those who are in pain and not yet whole, we surround ourselves with Light, see the Light that is within them, and give from open hearts that have some savvy about protection. True hospitality is not about being a doormat; it's about knowing when to open the door.

Your experiences of ordinary life will be greatly enhanced when all is well with your soul. Spiritual transformation benefits the challenges of daily life. Of course, it is not all sweetness and light to get there. Sometimes, maybe depending on how hard-headed we are, we go through challenging experiences on journeys in order to get to the healing. Once I journeyed with the request, "Please take me to a teacher who will help me survive this loss." A myriad of changes in my life had me in a maelstrom of depressive grief. I narrowed my intention to a very specific need, medicine to make it through.

> My power animal appeared immediately. He led me to a
> cemetery. The headstones were old. I saw a gray skeleton.
> "Are you my teacher?"
>
> "Your teacher is death."

"Am I going to die?" I looked into his hollow eyes.

"Not now. But this place, this burial ground, is your teacher."

The sky was gray, streaked with black. I was surrounded by swirling clouds. "Do I need to bury things?"

The skeleton told me solemnly that I would need to let go of a lot. "You need to sit in the presence of death and not die."

It was very quiet here. I knew I'm to hibernate in this cave in the presence of death and not die. I wasn't too scared. Though it was a barren place, the skeleton seemed cordial enough. "Will this go on forever?"

"No," the skeleton replied. "Death goes on forever. You are very much in life. The graves sustain you in ways you don't understand."

I shuddered. "I feel very alone."

The skeleton smiled. "That is the lesson. You are very alone and will one day die. You will seem to lose everything, yet life will be more precious. You will learn to live deeply in each moment, present and alive. You'll never return to your old ways."

His teaching barely seeped into my gloom but I lived into its profound truth. I was given the medicine of hope. I knew from that day I would survive and as more journeys brought healing, I eventually was filled to the brim with vitality and joy. Blessed.

Blessed. To be blessed is to have awareness of Spirit at work in one's life. To know that one's angels, ancestors and guides are at work to bring Light, guidance and healing at all times. A blessing involves the powers of heaven at work on our behalf.

May our blessing be that we live in harmony with our spirit helpers, in loving connection with our inner circle of beloveds, in respect and good will toward the large community, in reverence to all creation and creatures, and that we find our path of service which most enhances our own creative spirits. As we grow in soul, our capacity to love flows from a fountain within that is truly bottomless. Love abounds. But wisdom and discretion must grow also. Sometimes anger is a good friend. Our anger at injustice of any kind, if it is in the service of love, is great fuel. We need not speak or act out of emotion but let the anger be the transformative energy which quickens our intentions and efforts to set things right. Anger has great clarifying power to move us along towards justice. It is unjust to treat others unkindly; it is unjust to treat ourselves unkindly.

I'm not sure any spiritual teaching will ever improve upon the motto I adopted as a child growing up, "Do unto others as you would have them do unto you." Those words were knit into my bones. But I would get worn out trying to meet other peoples' needs, trying to accommodate what others wanted from me. And it was made doubly hard because I could sense unspoken needs. Sometimes that verse didn't serve me well because you can "do unto others" out of a pretty empty tank if you don't "do unto you" with love and respect. We must open the valves of our heart to the spiritual power that wants to flow through and honor above all else our connection to Spirit. Out of that integrity, "Doing unto others" is a path of service grounded in wellbeing.

I always used to think it was a good idea to live in the present, but I didn't know how to do it. Unconsciously, I was still carrying unfinished business from the past. I didn't have enough trust in myself or Spirit to live joyfully into the future. My visits to the spirit world have brought me squarely into the present.

## INVITATION

Play the xylophone, the harmonica.
Take off your shoes, dance in the dirt.
Take off your clothes, run through the sprinkler.
Remove the gloss, the watches, the schedules.
Be with the birds, the flowers, the trees.
Earth explodes in color and ease.
Spirits everywhere
Invite us to play,
Tease us into life.

You are invited to a party,
a celebration made ready since the beginning time.
Let the healing begin.
Join the dance
of spirit world and human world
engaged in ecstasy.

Walk through the looking glass.
Fall down the tunnel.
Be Alice in wonderland,
Barbara in wonderment,
Fern in wonder,
You are invited to explore
and bring others along.

Come from there to here
then to now
form to spirit
material to spiritual
apparent to real
limit to limitless
space to boundless
time to eternity

SHARON BLESSUM

Live from the now
into the larger NOW
in which ALL is present HERE.
You are surrounded by all possibilities.
Hold up the antennae of your heart.
Draw into yourself the substance and sustenance of Spirit.
All is here for us.

Spirit Homes

S

I grew up on the prairies. I remember the wide blue skies and the frequent fluffy clouds that carried images for me. I remember walking through the hot wheatfields, the stubble that stung my legs and the grasshoppers jumping everywhere. I remember the weeping birch tree in the yard. I'd lean against it for hours, watching bugs in the grass, reading, or gazing at the big lilac bush when it bloomed. I'd fill my bedroom with those purple flowers. That fragrance is the dearest of the year to me. Even now, two thousand miles away and decades later, I can place myself under that birch tree and send my soul into the center of that lilac bush. It's innards are like a hearth.

You have places like that too. A spirit home. Your spirit home is that place in nature where you sit on the edge between two worlds, a place of threshold where you find natural portals to another dimension. Your spirit home might be a garden, mountaintop, seaside, childhood tree, forest, prairie, canyon, your own backyard.

Remember lying in the grass and looking up into the sky? We are called into altered consciousness. Nature provides endless openings to the spirit world.

If you want to visit your spirit home, you only need the intention. And your intention can include the commitment to yourself and Spirit that nothing harmful will happen to you.

After you have read the next two paragraphs, lie down and close your eyes. It helps to cover your eyes. Relax your body so it can gratefully go off duty. Mentally scan your whole body to be sure it is released into stillness. You might like to use a shamanic drumming tape, for the monotonous percussive sound has been used for tens of thousands of years to help humans alter their state of consciousness. These ancient disciplines still the senses and enable the soul to fly. If that is not your way, play meditative music. Or, be in silence. Make an agreement with yourself that when the drumbeat on the tape changes to a callback, or when ten to fifteen minutes have passed, you will come back through the portal, to your spirit home, then into your body. And open your eyes.

After you close your eyes, and relax your body, you say, "I'm going to discover my spirit home." Maybe several scenes will appear to you. Gently, let one rise to the surface. See yourself in that spirit home where you find quiet and calm—that place where the rest of the world seems to fall away. Then, immerse yourself in the sights, smells and sounds of that special sanctuary. Allow yourself to be still. In your spirit home in nature, look for an opening to appear to you. Maybe you will see a knothole in a tree, a bubble in the lake, a cave in the mountain, a fissure in a rock, a cleft in a blade of grass. Pass through the portal. Choose the road not taken.

On the other side of the portal is the spirit world, a realm of wonder. For now, just explore this sacred landscape. The more you can give yourself to this experience the more you will feel refreshed when you return to ordinary consciousness. When you return, write about it . . . .

In the Dakotas we lived for the harvest. The golden carpets stretched out under the summer sun, waving their ripeness to those who tend the land. I spent many Augusts sitting in the cab of the truck waiting for my dad's combine to come around the corner, watching for his cue for me to pull the truck alongside so the grain could spew through the chute into the back of the truck.

One summer, I remember reading the Psalms while I waited. Favorites still come to companion me:

> *"As a hart longs for flowing streams, so longs my soul for thee, O God." Ps. 42:1*

> *"Take delight in God and you will be given the desires of your heart." Ps. 37:4*

> *"The Lord is my shepherd, I shall not want. . . ." Ps. 23:1*

What hours were portals for you as a teenager? When and where did you go out into nature to be alone with yourself, free from family and friends so your soul could listen?

Again, return to your spirit home, pass through the portal, and state this intention: I want to journey to the memory of that location where my soul was nurtured as a youth, to hear a psalm or song that nurtured me. After your return back through your spirit home into your body and into your room, open your eyes and write what was given you:

When you are ready, close your eyes again, ask for a new psalm to be given you, a song to guide your way this day:

In the winter, my dad would get out his little tractor and clear the yard. Mountains of snow were left for my sisters and me to play on. Some of those days when I played in the snow piles, I'd build stages and then create plays on them until my nose froze and all the scarves mom had wrapped around me couldn't keep me warm anymore. "Let's pretend" and the use of imagination were wonderful parts of my life and have been a strong blessing as I recovered their gifts in adulthood. It is our imaginations that build the snow piles from which Spirit takes us into flight. Then we go on adventures that are more than imagination. We know it's not just imagination because of the profound changes that transform our lives when we get on our spiritual path.

Pass through the portal of your spirit home with the intention, "Spirit, take me to a stage and roles I created as a child where I can find nourishment for my life now." Then, write it....

s

Now close your eyes again and travel to a future stage, asking Spirit to show you an environment conducive to your soul's growth and the role you are to take . . . .

One of my clients had been experiencing a lot of chest pain from overwhelming anxiety. Sometimes she felt so small and life's challenges felt so big. She had come a long way on her healing path and felt discouraged by these dark feelings. She knew the pains were not dangerous, yet they planted worries about her health. I journeyed into the spirit world to ask for healing for her. First I saw a dark shelf of energy above her heart. When that toxicity was all removed, a nest was planted in her heart. A beautiful nest. Then I saw a little bird in the nest being fed. Like the child in her, nourished by the Greatmother. I saw the little bird flourish, fly off, and return to rest in the nest. Rest in the Nest. Rest in the Nest. That phrase was a gift to her and filled her heart as we talked after the healing. Because she is adept at spiritual work, she felt immediate relief and did not experience the overwhelming pressure in her chest again. She began to see the nest in her heart and to know that place as home. Her home. Within her. Safe. Nothing in the world could get her there.

Our spirit homes are like nests in our heart. As we see the scene from which we move into the spirit world, we are rendered peaceful as babes at mother's breast. We are safely ensconced in the place where cares fall away. Visiting our spirit homes gives us access to unlimited healing and guidance.

Close your eyes again and return to your spirit home. Let it become a nest in your heart. Rest in the nest. Rest in the fullness of this oasis where your soul is nurtured. Don't journey further this time, just be at the portal where the worlds meet. Your sacred space. Then, write about it....

Guides

$A$s you follow the path further into the spirit world, you will become aware of spirit beings around you. It is not that you have to travel toward them; they are always around you. It is only a matter of altering your consciousness so you can be aware of them. They are attuned to you; you can be attuned to them. There are animals, angels, ancestors, teachers, guides who bring help. They have enormous compassion for us on our earthwalk and serve Spirit by serving us.

In the experiences of this chapter we will become more aware of who surrounds us, for we are not alone. It is helpful to use the same process throughout this book. Your spiritual practice will deepen as you follow the same pathways. Our practice is modeled after shamanic journeys. (As a shamanic practitioner, I hate to compare a process learned in a book to shamanism. Much that is called shamanism today is not. This ancient tradition is powerful and demanding. Yet, access to the spirit world is not only for the 'technicians of the sacred', but also for ordinary people who long for this connection.)

We always begin lying down or sitting comfortably with drumbeat or music which calls our soul on its journey. We close our eyes, go to our familiar spirit home and pass through the luminous portal into a greater consciousness. If you do it the same way each time, you will get to know the neighborhood!

Remember the importance of intentions. This time, when you travel into the spirit world, you state an intention to meet your power animal. Power animals are like guardian angels. Some cultures say they are assigned to us at birth to protect us. They are friendly spirits. Maybe you've had a lifelong connection to a kin-dred spirit and you won't be surprised at who shows up. But be open to a truly unexpected animal. Let mystery reveal itself. Know that your power animal is one of the oldest friends you have in the spirit world. Maybe you will see many animals pass in front of your inner eye, but one will become predominant. Or maybe there will be only one, who shows you a whole variety of scenes in which that animal is present. Allow yourself to experience the awareness of this animal whose only purpose seems to be to love you and companion you. When the power animal has made itself known to you, invite this animal to journey back with you through the open-ing into your spirit home. Further, invite the animal to return with you into your ordinary world to walk your walk with you, to bring you protection and power.

Then begins a mutual dance of friendship. The more you honor the presence and power of this invisible friend, the more this friend will bring you energy from the other side. You will be blessed.

In true shamanic cultures, the retrieval of one's power animal is a sacred healing. When there are illnesses or injuries, power animals may seem unavailable. Shamans journey into the spirit world on behalf of another to recover their animal and reunite them. Because animals spirits are a universal part of the spiritual experience, we, too, can approach this holy relationship. Be aware this is a time-honored tradition to be done with humility and gratitude. If you live near a shamanic practitioner, it would be worth having that person do this journey for you. But if not, no one need be deprived. Journey from your spirit home into the spirit world with the intention to meet your power animal and bring it joyfully into your conscious awareness. Write about what happens . . . .

After you and your animal friend have settled into each other, you will want to know each other. This spirit is like a new best friend, a true ally in this world and the other. Invite your power animal to be with you on your daily rounds, to live with you, to protect you, and to be a part of your life. As part of your bonding, honor the animal by a photograph or sacred object or ritual that demonstrates your love.

Your animal companion in the spirit world can become very dear to you. He or she can be of very powerful assistance in your earthwalk. And from now on, this companion should accompany you on all of your visits to the spirit world. It doesn't matter if this is a dog, cat, elephant, snake, winged creature or amphibian. It will be able to fly, swim, and go everywhere it is needed, for it is constituted by energy in a less dense way than you are and can travel freely in the energy field of Spirit. In the spirit world, your spirit animal will know more than you about where you need to visit and what spirit teachers you need to meet on a particular day. In the ordinary world, your animal is a fine guardian in challenging experiences such as job interviews, dental visits, surgery, etc. If you can close your eyes and have the Great Shaman Jesus holding your hand and your power animal patroling the boundaries of your energy field, you are in good company!

Now, journey back into the spirit world with your animal friend asking the animal to show you more of itself, its traits, its gifts, that you might become more intimate with this companion. Write about what happens . . . .

Spirit guides, teachers and healers, travel at our side at times. Their home is the spirit realm and they have their own life, but they are available to us and seem most ready to be on call. They have great compassion and love for us. Our honoring of them is good for them and us.

Today, you journey into the spirit world to invite a primary spirit guide to show up, to teach you and to begin a conscious relationship which will be with you for all of your days. The spirit guide may be a very ordinary figure, a well-known religious figure such as Mary or Jesus, a goddess, a Native American shaman, an ancestor. Usually the guide is of more anonymous origins, but of powerful knowing.

If you are concerned about meeting dark spirits, you need to know that you can always protect yourself from that experience. You and the Great Spirit can have a covenant about that. You can ask your power animal to allow only beneficent spirits around you. You can invoke a tent of sacred and safe Light whenever you do your spiritual work. It is important to know that you are working in a realm of enormous powers. I almost didn't write this book because of my awe and respect for the shamanic tradition. I don't want to be part of diluting such a venerable tradition and I don't believe in dabbling in the spirit world. Shamanism is not a parlor game; it is an ancient practice of enormous power. This book is but a baby step into the vast ocean of possibility. It is the merest drop of the great waters and I humbly acknowledge that. However, I am also bold to invite you to this practice knowing that it may help you on your healing path, and may lead you to a community of like-minded people. You may not go on into true shamanic work but you will have greater resource for your spiritual work.

Go to your spirit home, ask your power animal to journey with you through a portal and take you to the spirit guide who wants to work with you at this time. Ask your guide to begin to teach you how you can work together so you can create the earthwalk of the greatest good for your soul. Write about it . . . .

s

Other helpers in the spirit world are ancestors. Today, as you rest in the nest of your spirit home and invite your power animal to be with you, travel into the spirit world to meet an ancestor who brings guidance and support to you. Do not predetermine who it is. You may meet someone you once knew here, who is now in spirit or maybe someone in your lineage, whom you have never heard of, will come. Just invite an ancestor who is spiritually evolved and wants to help you with your life. When they show up, thank them for their presence and learn what gifts, wisdom or healing they bring you. Ask how to better know them and honor them. Afterwards, write....

Many years ago I was journeying for my own healing. I was very sad. I had lost many familiar pillars that held me securely in life and was bereft and frightened. Anchorless. My spirit guide came to me day after day with wisdom and compassion. She knew more about what I was going through than I did and her words were a beacon in the dark, a light onto my path. This particular day my grief sliced through my body in unyielding strokes. In the middle of the journey my spirit guide asked if I would like to see my mother.

My mother had left this earth many years earlier. I missed her and longed for the opportunity to bring peace to unresolved issues between us; but that was long ago and I had truly never thought of her in relation to a shamanic journey.

When I was asked if I wanted to see her, the tears that had been running down my face stopped in shock as I took in the words. "Yes, yes, I would like to see her." She appeared and I knew immediately that she was well.

"I am more your mother than ever before," she said. "You can come to me; all has healed between us."

She went on to tell me about her progress in soul and then began to bestow great gifts upon me. She told me things I didn't know about her and about me. She gave me a love unlike anything I had ever known.

I wouldn't have known how to make this up. And if I did, I'd have done it ten years sooner when I was in fresh loss of her. She came entirely unbidden, pure gift of Spirit. Our visits continued till I was completely imbued with her love for me. She continues to visit me at times when I could use support. Once I felt her hand on my shoulder when I was at a funeral.

The last few years I have experienced unexplainable events on her birthday. And when I started this writing, for the first time ever, my ears heard an audible voice say, "That's wonderful." The room was empty but I think it was her. I am indebted to her for life and possibility. As my love and honoring of her grew, I suspect a way was paved for the GreatMother who showed up later in journeys and now is at the center of my self and service.

My mother's visits were not only my first exposure to connection with ancestors, but also began a way for me to help others connect with their ancestors. Many people have shed tears of joy at workshops as they are surprised by the presence of a loved one lost long gone. These ancestors still love us! We are so much more loved than we realize. That is what this work is all about. Once we know how loved we are, we can never be the same. There is great power at work on our behalf.

We also have angels who seem assigned to us. Angels appear in many forms. For now, we will invite the presence of a luminous being who wants to help you live in fullness of soul. Follow your now familiar route into the spirit world calling for an angel to meet you. Welcome the warm, golden glow that comes when the angel shows up. Meet in that radiant energy. When you are ready, invite that angel to take you on an adventure, with the promise that when you are finished, you will return safely to your spirit home, then your body, then your ordinary life. Write about your visit . . . .

I will never forget one spirit guide who surprised me. Yikes! (This teacher is a good reminder that sometimes spirits show up who would scare us in ordinary consciousness but who are quite acceptable in the spirit world. However, if we ever meet a spirit that feels ominous, we can turn away. We always have free choice in both states of consciousness.)

Still in the sad, scary, long, dark night of the soul, I journeyed daily with loving helpers who soothed and guided me. But one day my power animal told me there was someone else down the path I was to meet. As we kept going, I felt chilly, increasingly cold and wet.

"AAAAAAAAH" a great growl sounded at the same moment I beheld a raging beast. At first I thought it was an angry lion, then a dragon, as I saw its big, wide, open mouth spewing fire. "I am your teacher," he screamed. "I am your teacher and I am about fire. WHERE IS YOUR FIRE?" His voice only got louder till the ground shook and I felt small and subdued. He was fiercer than a dragon, this dragoon.

In my littlest voice I offered, "You want my anger, don't you?"

"YESSSSSS" he bellowed back. "I want you to know that you cannot tolerate being treated as less than you are. You deserve MOOOOOOORE." He went on and on, then scolded me. "You deserve to be treasured. You gave your gold away. You are made of gold."

"I am made of gold?" I queried.

As I sensed his impatience, I said it again without the question. "I am made of gold."

s

"Say it louder," he said. I did; he still wasn't satisfied. We went on and then he said, "I am here to heal you. Do you want to be healed?"

"Yes." But before the word was out I knew he had me. If I were healed I'd have to grow up and away from the only security I had left to hold on to. I'd have to get big.

"Do you want to be healed?" he reiterated. He asked me over and over till I screamed at him.

"YES. I want to be HEEEEEEEEEALD." Then he was satisfied.

So I, who felt I had lost everything, was confronted by this dark angel who told me I must lose even more till I had ONLY my soul to cling to and then only would I be healed.

"Stop being abused by what is going on. You have to protect yourself. You need to know your own fullness with or without all you have lost. You need to be BIG."

My power animal and I had many visits to this being I call a dragoon, and my healing is absolutely indebted to his confrontations. He insisted that I get a bigger self. Little by little, I did.

Much later, when this dragoon's teaching had been fully integrated into my life, I remembered that when I was a young girl my mother used to tell me that I had a heart made of gold. Thank you, dragoon, for helping me recover part of myself lost in limbo years ago.

I've long kept Marianne Williamson's words by my bathroom mirror:

Your playing small doesn't serve the world. There's nothing enlightened about shrinking so that other people won't feel insecure around you. You were born to make manifest the glory of God that is within you.

It's not just in some of us; it's in everyone. And as you let your light shine, you unconsciously give other people permission to do the same.

In our drumming circle, we are aware that one person's growth enhances us all. As someone begins a new course, takes her paintings to a gallery, publishes an article, becomes a grandmother, leaves or begins a marriage, starts a business, we are there to support that person's venture toward bigness. We also experience that when one person keeps herself small in circle, we all feel the energy drain. We learn a lot by sitting in circle. We are healed and we are empowered. We are aware that our spirit guides are also gathered around and among us. They rejoice in our growth.

The Path

Owl
bows
to the
Path

When I was growing up I thought there was something wrong with me, that everybody but me knew what it was; but I didn't. If I only knew what it was, I'd fix it. I also wished I was like everybody else. I seemed so serious and sensitive compared to everyone else. In addition, I had the same lack of self esteem that most girls have by adolescence. Deep suffering came with the sense of being different, which now has been healed by the gratitude of being who I am. I am grateful to be me. Filled with joy. Blessed by Spirit. Many other people felt the same way I did. Only I didn't know it and they didn't know it, so we each felt very alone and strange. My clients work on this issue frequently. We had false information about who we were.

If you have ever felt odd and inadequate, not honoring your unique path you might like to journey to a spirit guide for healing. Write what happens . . . .

My favorite quote in college was Thoreau's famous encouragement to march to one's own drummer.

In the conformity of college
I sigh
when Thoreau breaks in with permission
to follow the drum I hear
though it leads me from the Dakota badlands
land of the straight and narrow
to questing decades
up mountains and down valleys
till the goodlands
claim my way
not confining
but configuring safety
in terrain that had seemed only rugged
I go home
with my own drum

When you follow your own drum, when you drum yourself into a state of being where the spirit world is your familiar home, you will value your solitary path and you will feel more at home in the world than ever. You'll be glad to be you! Yet, even though your love for this sensory world grows, you will also be aware that this is not your true home, that you are a visitor here. Home is not where you hang your hat but where your soul resides. That realm offers you spiritual guidance and healing while you visit this wondrous earthplane.

As you become increasingly openhearted on your earthwalk, you will find yourself courted by spirits. One of the lovely ways this happens is in the gifting of feathers. Spirits must have quite an intimate connection with birds because feathers seem to appear like miracles on people's paths—often when they most need encouragement, and often in the most unusual places. One man, the morning after he'd been here for a shamanic healing, opened his wallet and found a tiny white feather in with his dollar bills. He had no explanation for that! Another woman, wooed by bluejay as her soul expanded, was doing dishes one midnight when she took the lid off a frying pan and there was a blue feather!

If you want to, you can journey to the giver of the feather you find and ask for its message to be made clear to you. Many people build little altars in their homes with feathers and found objects in nature that bring blessing and connection. However, they do not remove natural items from places of beauty when it is obvious those stone or limbs belong where they are!

Say yes to the path
let the path lead you
you don't lead the path
for it has better places to go
than your imagination knows

or

say no
and stay where you are

there is more at work in the world than you
you don't have to make anything happen
prepare your heart
and let the gifts of life come in

there is a goodness and a power in the universe
at work on your behalf
plant your feet firmly
on this belief

in the time of unknowing
you are
all right
live more deeply in the inner
trust the outer to fall into place

es

let the outside manifest the inside
instead of the reverse

sink your roots into the earth
She will sustain your being


give up the future
there is no future
today is yours
mine for gold

Journey to a spirit guide with the intention to find help to discern your true path. Write about it . . . .

Spirit erupts in earthly forms
say hello to your sister and brother,
mountains, mourning doves, rocks, rain
and all others
who nod to you on your path.
Angels walk among you.

You will find messages everywhere to guide your path. Journey to a spirit guide to ask illumination about some issue that needs clarity in order for you to take the next step on your path. Write . . . .

You have a gift to give this world just by being you. And NO ONE ELSE can give that gift. *You are the only you there is.* If I could look deep into your eyes, I know I would travel through the tunnel to light and see the signature of your soul that is unique and beloved to Spirit. I see in the realm around you, beings who have compassion for you, ancestors who want to bring guidance, animals and angels who are supporting you. You are not alone. I can see that. *I salute you.* I would wish for you to find the meaning of your life as well as the comfort and courage which are needed a part of each day.

Blessing

is

to sing

to sing your song

your whole life long

Look with soft vision toward a tree, a cloud, or a flower in your field of vision. Visit the spirit of that lifeform to receive a song of blessing....

Now, let yourself experiment with stating an intention on some issue which is a challenge on your path. It might be a relationship, a job, an event in the past, a fear or anxiety. Close your eyes and open your vision to your spirit home. Rest in the nest till you are ready to pass into that world where your guides await you. Remember to state your intention clearly. "I'm going into the spirit world with my power animal to seek healing or guidance about . . . ." If you ever feel distracted, just restate your intention. It really helps our focus to say the whole journey out loud. When you are finished, thank your guides and return through that familiar portal, to your spirit home, into your body, opening your eyes, and then write . . . .

s

We are part of the natural world and have kinship with all that is. Nature is an intimate companion in this earthwalk and can truly offer guidance to your path. You are not in some foreign territory, the way it feels, but in a temporary homeland that wants to provide sustenance and support to you. Let the luminous journeys lead you to abundance.

You can lie down, cover your eyes, turn on a drumming tape and state an intention to meet with the spirit of a cloud. Or, you can walk outside with soft vision with the intention to receive messages from a cloud in the sky or to read messages written in a rock. In either process, you are in a state of altered consciousness and open to Spirit's message that comes directly to your soul. Your intuitive capacity is being sharpened; your inner eye is more open to see, your ear to hear, your heart to know. You know how to meet the essence of a rock or tree. You can hear the songs, see the spirits, learn the lessons, and experience connectedness. Hold a stone you treasure or go outside and sit next to a rock that calls to you. Ask for its message . . . .

Trees, the tall people, constantly talk to us. Around my little farm, bare branches, like antlers, reach into the sky as antennae for Spirit. Like lightning rods, they call in the power to protect and embrace this land. What sentinels around your home offer similar service to you?

The large tree that had creaked and groaned in December finally fell over. A cedar had provided hospice for a long time but a strong wind eventually prevailed. It blocked the front of the shed in the far back, hurting nothing. Cathy came over with her chain saw in tow (and Jack!) and took care of it, toting the pieces of the tree out to the back where other fallen ones lay in grace and beauty. I went out and saw the new logs lying among the limbs of their ancestors. I found myself singing to them, blessing them and thanking them for the blessing they were to the Farm.

The cemetery of ancestors in the back has often welcomed me to its land of form-beyond-death. Though the trees are bare and their bodies finished, their spirits rustle in the air, still teaching me. They are bathed in Light. Much calm.

Many tree persons befriend us on our earthwalk. Some stand sentry to our comings and goings, friendly companions. Some speak. Some offer shade. Many teach us through the cycles of the year and guide us through our own passages.

Various cultures and individuals have found the World Tree at the portal to the spirit world. Ask your power animal to take you to that power tree. Journey through the roots of the tree to learn about being grounded for when you need the strength of rootedness in your life. Or into its trunk or branches or leaves if you want their teachings. Write about it . . .

S

Go outside with soft vision and ask to be guided to a tree that wants to befriend you. Let yourself follow, not lead, and when you near the tree, approach it with reverence. As you honor its presence, it will respond to you and give you a song. Learn the song this tree wants to teach you . . . .

Think of an issue in your life that could benefit from the wisdom of tree spirits. Travel through the luminous portal that is the knothole, into the secrets and systems of the tree where you can find guidance . . . .

Journey to the center of a tree and ask a symbol to be revealed that could help you with your life at this time. Receive it as a gift . . . .

Your experiences with tree spirit can be expanded to flowers, clouds, mountains, rivers, etc.

Nature is our friend, our physical home, in this ordinary world. Nature also provides passages for us to enter other dimensions of reality. The four elements offer enormous help to us on our earthwalk. We honor their medicine in the medicine wheel and in many other spiritual practices. Know that Earth, Air, Water, and Fire can truly help you with your path.

# EARTH

Earth invites us in. Ashes to ashes, dust to dust, we shall return. In the meantime, throughout life, the warm wombs of the Earthmother offer warmth, solace, and protection. We come from Her womb, hide in Her grasses, eat from Her bounty, drink from Her streams, smile at Her flowers, climb Her trees, explore Her caves, and finally, rest our bones in Her depths. Earth, our GreatMother, births us and sustains us all our days, receives us at the end of our days. She is beautiful, lush, powerful, full of nourishment. Our relationship to Her ranges from mastery and control (the great illusion) to reverence and honor. To the extent we honor Her, and cooperate with Her energies, we thrive. To the extent we bring harm to Her, we bring suffering upon nature and ourselves.

Many luminous portals exist in the earth's body—caves, craters, gullies, gorges, from the smallest molehole to the largest canyon. We are invited in. Journey with the intention to meet a spirit teacher who will take you to a special cave or unknown place to teach you about your relationship to earth. Perhaps, this will be the first of many journeys with this teacher.

Write about your lessons...

s

Journey into the spirit world with the intention to ask if there are any beliefs or behaviors in you that are in the way of having a good relationship with Earth. Ask for this to be revealed and healed. Write about it . . . .

# AIR

Air is our necessary companion throughout our life. Air fills our lungs and outer space. Air holds the mysteries of light and dark, the patterns of winds, the accumulations of rain and snow. Sky is the home to moon and sun. Sky calls us to angels and ancestors. Sky reminds us that we are small and tells us that we are big. The winds blow where they will and we learn from their currents.

Before we go any further, take a peek out your window or if you are outside, look up, and take in the presence of your old friend Sky. Take in deep breaths of air. Feel the breezes on your skin. Let Air know that you want to be more aware of your relationship.

"In the beginning God created the heavens . . . and God said, 'Let there be light' and there was light. And God saw it was good; and God separated the light from the darkness. God called the light day and the darkness Night."

Increase your awareness of the portals in the sky or the lessons of the wind. You have known them all your life. How I used to love lying in the grass and looking up into those North Dakota skies which stretch endlessly. Cloud choreography was different every day! I'd recognize shapes, watch them disperse, and wait for the next amazing sight.

we ride
the great tao
through the panorama of life

The sky offers a palette
to you
woos you with wild colors
to wrap yourself in

Draw down the sunset
paint your life with it

Choose your brushstrokes carefully
for the very air wears
your garments

In shamanic journeys, the sky is often a reminder of the upper world, the realms of angels and ancestors, the ethers in which great teachers and healers appear. Give yourself a new experience by going to your spirit home and then looking for an opening that will lead you up this time, up into the lightness of being where a new kind of adventure is evoked. Maybe you will gather at the heart of Mary, or meet a loved one on the other side, or come face to face with the angel who has long attended you. Your intention for this first journey is simply to travel into the upper realms of the spirit world to meet a teacher who would like to work with you. Write what happens . . . .

Lift again into the upper realms and ask to meet a spirit guide who will give you a song or a poem to help you open to the grace of that place. Write it...

Many times my dad will go out into the evening air, before going to bed, and look at the starry night. He'll then come in and say, "It's a large evening." That's how I learned what large is.

meet me in the meadow
where we can scrye the sky
and let the clouds teach us
of days gone by
when we were little sisters
lying in the grass
filled with the skill
to let time pass
I want those days back
of resting in the sun
not waiting till it's too late
who cares if the work's all done

We keep ourselves small when we do not breathe in the wonders of the sky. Being able to journey into the spiritual realms of the upper regions, we are able to experience one of the great lessons of the upper world, which is a new perspective on our life "below." We look into our human plane with increasing compassion and awareness. We look into the upper realms with gratitude and ecstasy. Those beings whose home is on the other side, whose vibration is different than ours, who come from the higher places, bring messages and ministry to us.

Journey again, now, into the upper world, through portals in the clouds to ask Spirit to teach you about those magical realms. Write about it . . . .

# WATER

Another friend, Water, draws us into eternal Being. Our mothers gave us our first home in the liquid safety of their wombs. From their bodies we took nourishment and possibility. Possibility of life itself. We grew and grew till the time for our passage out into the world. The wombwaters were our introduction to buoyant goodness.

Take yourself to your familiar spirit home and ask your spirit guide to escort you back through time and space to your mother's womb. Your intention is to learn all you can of that prenatal experience, even sensing energy states in your mother, and to see for yourself the identity of that soul that was coming into life. Let Spirit guide you. Then, write....

Water is a great resource in both worlds. We know that a large percentage of our body is composed of water. We know we need to drink water to live. We are aware of water as a great cleanser, purifier. We wash our hands, shower our bodies. It's all so obvious. So, it is not surprising that part of the series of my own healing journeys led me to the waters of a temple:

> I walk up the steps to a small, lovely temple. I proceed into the atrium, and see a pool with beautiful tiling around it. The room looks luminous. I take off my clothes and lie down in the water. There is no one there with me now, no one. I float, held up by the water, suspended and soothed. THE WATER IS HOLDING ME.
>
> I open my eyes. Tiles shine, beautiful colors, blues and turquoises. Green plants line the round room.

I stand up and a woman appears. She takes my hand as I step out of the water and puts a white towel around me. We sit inside on two short benches beside a window. The window faces out to trees. A slight breeze comes in, warm.
She says, "I am here to tell you that as this part of your life ends, you will not drown. You will be held up by the water."

"There is so much loss," I utter.

"Yes, there is loss . . . let yourself be held up by the waters. Your healing will bring you into your full light and wisdom. Do not be held back from who you can be." She speaks as one who knows.

I respond, "I feel like a child who wants to bask in mother love."

My wise teacher nods at me. "Yes, that is the tenderest gift one human being ever gives another. But no one can do that better than you. Find the mother love in your own heart and give it to yourself. Look into the mirror every day with the maternal gaze that feeds your soul."

I start to protest in fear, in tears. "But I need . . ."

Reluctantly, I'm taking in the truth of what she says.

"Your safekeeping cannot be in anyone else's hands. Only your own."

"I know I must learn that I will not die as I sustain this great loss, that I can nurture myself. Death is the great abandonment."

"You must not abandon yourself. That is the great death."

The woman by the waters met me many times as I was immersed in healing waters. I already had plenty of psychological insight about these matters, but the experience of the water was absolutely healing. As you are finding, spiritual experiences are far more powerful and life-changing than the insight of thought or the working through of feeling. Spirit is POWERFUL.

Another time I was led to the waters when I was journeying for forgiveness. I needed to be "reborn" from self-censure. As you know, forgiving ourselves is the hardest.

> I am led to the temple. I take my clothes off, lie down in the waters face up. I ask the waters to forgive me.
>
> I'm gently pressed down all the way till my face and entire body are immersed. I bob right back up to the surface. I turn over and go under again and slide down the drain.
>
> Down through the drain, I come out into immense sunlight. A circle of beings forms around me, vague, lightbeings that I can't see clearly. I can tell they have arms and hands because they now connect in a circle around me, placing me in the center. I can see their shapes.
>
> "Are you my teachers?" I say. They start to hum.
>
> "Are you the ones to bring me forgiveness for my failures?" Their humming is louder. "Will you be teaching me to hum, to chant?" Their chanting gets louder. Their chanting surrounds me and I know that I am accepted, forgiven.

That hum, of course, became so loud that it now reverberates throughout my life. My way of being changed.

One day, when doing a journey for someone else, I was taken to the familiar waters to witness and evoke a healing for my client. Her self-hate had made her a magnet for toxic energy.

Someone appears with a wire brush and scrubs abrasively against the women's skin. I wince. She doesn't bleed but sloughs off dead skin and grime. My power animal stands at a discreet distance. Now it's soap suds. Same hard brush, though. She's being scrubbed again, lathered and scrubbed, lathered and scrubbed. Every crevice being scrubbed, even under her nails. A long time passes.

When the healing was over, new soft skin appeared as a sign she had been restored to her original beauty. Our original beauty is what was present in the womb before our journey out. Sometimes life is very hard and the human condition is very challenging, so we lose sight of our splendor.

Now, ask your spirit helpers to bring a wounded part of you to healing waters. Maybe you will be immersed in loving waters, soothed and quieted by a gentle pond, cleansed by a running stream, tossed about and made new by the ocean. Let it happen and then write about it...

# FIRE

Fire is our friend. About once a month my drumming circles do a fire ceremony as part of our spiritual maintenance. We journey into the spirit world and ask our guides to reveal any toxic energy that needs to be removed. Depending on what themes we are working on, we might ask for release of an old memory, an emotional block, a relationship that needs closure, etc. But we don't predetermine what particular item will show up regarding one of those themes. We let Spirit show us what we need to know, of which we might not be conscious. After the journeys, we sit in a circle and drum in slow motion while one person approaches the altar in the center. Silently, the person tells the fire what needs to be burned away. We use a little toothpick to comb the energy field around us to help collect and remove any unhealthy residue that has been clinging to us, then we put the "little log" into the fire. The rest of us speed up our drumming as witness and support to the person's healing. She takes her place back in the circle and then someone else comes up to the fire.

Fire brings release, transformation of energy. Sacred fires burn away psychic trash, refine us down to our core. Fire ceremonies exist in many cultures. I have experienced them in large drumming circles that gathered around an outdoor blaze where fifty of us drummed for three hours. I have experienced a different version as a young girl in a Lutheran church where we wrote sins we wanted forgiven on a sheet of paper and then burned them. The fire helps us burn, shed, let go of toxic energy. The fire transforms the negative energy so that no harm comes from it toward any life forms. Room is made for the new. Talking or reading about it sounds weak compared to the strength of the real ritual.

I worked intensively with a woman who wanted to die, who was ready to help herself out of this world. I sat vigil at her death wish for all too long. Eventually, she became interested in spiritual healing and that gave me an opportunity to work with Spirit on her behalf. One day in a session, I journeyed for her. I was introduced to Fire as friend and healer:

I sit by a fire in a wonderful round room. Many people are in the shadows of the room, paying no attention to one another as they do their work. Some chant, some drum, some journey. Many souls are working on the healing of depression.

The fire begins to speak. "I WILL BURN AWAY WHAT-EVER IS HAUNTING, DEPRESSING, HOLDING DOWN THE SOUL FROM ITS FULL LIFE. BRING ME WHAT IS TO BE BURNED AWAY. BRING ME TATTERED PIECES OF PAPER THAT LIST THE PAINS OF THE PERSON. LET ME BURN THE REM-NANTS OF THAT SUFFERING."

The fire gets hot, flames shoot up and I back away. The fire is like a campfire but crackles loud and burns hard as if it could take care of anything. "May I offer some to you now?" I ask.

"Yes."

I approach the fire with little pieces of paper which seem to carry messages about Ella's physical abuse and abandon-ment by her mother. Her body has long been holding the accumulative energy of those formative years, which by now has made her physically ill. On the papers are ailments and terror. I sprinkle them into the fire and hundreds more pa-pers join the others that I release from my hands. The flames rage up and I leap back.

There's more, more, more. The fire is weighed down by the papers of this ritual. Then the flames come way up, consuming these papers. I see the face of Ella smiling. I'm told this needs to be done three more times.

Because I work so much with women survivors of abuse, I ask, "Fire, what else do you want to tell me? How can people be healed?" I open the palms of my hands toward the spirit found in the fire. "Teach me . . . ."

"By burning the issues, as you just did. By giving to the fire or to the waters, bringing their suffering to us sacred elements, for we can transform the energy so people can have a new life."

I think of Maryellen and the sexual abuse that led to serious depression. My hands fill with notes of things she's told me. I rain those pieces of paper into the fire. The fire gets hot, flames shoot up and again I jump back.

"What else do I need to tell people about healing of the soul?"

Fire replied, "That it can be done, it can always be done on this side of death. As long as a person is alive, there is possibility for soul healing. But it does depend on that person's wanting it to happen. If there is enough longing for the soul in the person, that healthy essence can always be retrieved. As old destructive energy is released, spiritual energy can be retrieved. But of course many of you need to be doing the retrievals. Medication doesn't retrieve. So you have much work to do."

Ella, Maryellen, and many others have benefited from journeys such as this. Their commitment to life is unquestionable now. You might like to become closer friends with Fire. Begin by lighting a candle. The candle is a small campfire, a symbol of Grandfather Fire, the Sun. Gaze into your candle as you prepare to journey into the spirit world. Then state your intention: "I would like to go into the spirit world to learn more about the healing powers of Fire, to experience its great gift to me." Afterwards, write about what happened . . . .

s

Another intention to bring to Fire's healing is to ask your spirit guide to show you when you have been in a fiery ordeal, when you have felt that you just couldn't put out the fires, that you were walking on coals, that you were burned up about something, or even worse, burned out. Let Spirit show you when fire has seemed a negative for you. Go to the spirit of Fire to ask for a healing of those times. Your spirit helper will be there to help. You may find that times when fire seemed like an enemy, raging through your life in uncontrollable ways, it was actually clearing a path for you to reach a different way of life. Maybe it was a blessing in disguise. Maybe it was a teacher. Or maybe it was about things external to you, as if an arsonist had been at work and now it's left for you to do the clean up. Whatever Spirit reveals to you, let the healing come. Write about it afterwards . . .

Now you are ready for a fire ceremony of your own. First, gather a little pile of toothpicks to represent logs. Place them in one pot and have another empty pot to burn them in. Light your candle. If you are fortunate enough to be using this book with a friend or a group, you will find power in their support. Journey through your luminous portal and ask your spirit helpers to reveal whatever memories, energies, burdens, you need to give to the sacred fire. Write what comes . . . .

Then, drum, chant, hum or pray while each member of the group silently approaches the flame. In a group, each person speaks to the fire silently while the others are in support. If you are doing this alone, speak silently to the fire of your candle. Tell the fire what you are releasing. Then take a toothpick and use the tiny log to comb your aura, to remove any toxic residue from your energy field. Let it go by burning the toothpick in the fire.

come toward the Fire
let It take all you have
and give you back your More

Journey back into the spirit world and ask Spirit to give you a gift, a word or symbol to place in your heart as a replacement for the negativity that was there. Write it, draw it, sing it, dance it . .

"The place on which you are standing is holy ground." An ancestor, Moses, is out tending his flock. An ordinary day. Extraordinary hour. A burning bush. Moses' consciousness is altered. Through this luminous portal he sees an angel in the flame. This spirit guide speaks. Moses is in the very presence of the Divine Mystery.

You, too, are told to take off your shoes for the place on which you stand is hallowed. When the eyes of our hearts are open, we will know that all ground is holy ground, every inch of our beloved earth is the body of Spirit. Earth Mother. In the meantime, we need to be stopped in our tracks, told to remove our footwear and watch for the angels.

The bush is not consumed because in the spirit world all is eternal. Laws of nature as we know them are suspended and energies are at work to bring glory and power. It is our task to show up, to slow down, to look with wonder at the natural portals that appear before us day after day if we have eyes to see.

This angel wanted to tell Moses that God knew of his suffering, that guidance was at hand, that the people were not alone but would be led to a land flowing with milk and honey. You are no less significant. Spirit wants your attention, wants you to know there are angels serving you, messengers that you are not alone, that your life path is not in isolation, that you can be called from darkness to light.

> "Take off your shoes . . ."
> when you approach
> the sacred fire
> in the center of each soul.
> Each heart holds a flame, a burning bush.

Journey to Fire as the Sacred Presence. Ask to be led out of any affliction and to be taken to the land of milk and honey. Then, write....

Another experience of Spirit as Fire in the scriptures appeared shortly after Jesus' departure from earth. Fire came "from heaven like the rush of a mighty wind . . . and there appeared to them tongues as of fire, distributed and resting on each one of them." The people gathered began to speak in tongues. Perhaps you, too, have been visited by an ecstasy that breaks forth in sounds, dance, or some utterly foreign expression. Be brave. Journey into the spirit world and ask a spirit guide to take you to the holy fires for an experience of ecstasy . . . .

# Healing

Before you continue in your own journaling and work with the natural portals that call you into the spirit world, it might be helpful to see where all this can lead. Spiritual medicine can bring remarkable healing.

Albert Schweitzer observed about healing that "Each patient carries his/her own doctor inside. They come to us not knowing this truth. We are at our best when we give the doctor who resides within each patient a chance to go to work." Michael Harner, the founder of The Foundation for Shamanic Studies, suggests that the shamanic practitioner is uniquely qualified to give "the doctor inside a chance to go to work." His program and the innovative work on soul retrieval by Sandra Ingerman have greatly influenced the place of soul retrieval and spiritual healing in our culture.

My own belief is that we are all born with soul, luminous, fresh from union with the Great Spirit. We are born into the human condition, which brings traumas, losses and intrusions, which threaten the essence of who we are. Most of us accommodate by developing a false self in response to the expectations of those around us. We hide and lose our real selves. At the cost of pleasing our parents and culture, we sacrifice a great deal. Our real self is buried. That choice is often protective, because our souls could not endure in the environment we are in. But out of that loss of our souls, we are empty, scared, alienated. We look to addictions, relationships, work, headtrips, acting out and acting in. You know the story of what we do.

One major way we defend ourselves against the pain to our psyche is by *disassociating*. Many of the wounds we endure in life can only be tolerated by the psychological defense of disassociation. We split off, meaning that a part of us "goes somewhere else". It is the psyche's brilliant capacity to maintain functioning.

But that part of us that splits off doesn't die. There isn't really such a thing as soul murder. Rather, there is *soul loss*. The part that goes away is part of our soul. The soul is *energy*, so it goes into the spirit world where it stays until it is safe to return. It is in the energy field and is available to be returned to us when we are ready to be whole.

We all experience soul loss. It is part of the human experience. Sometimes it is dramatic, sometimes subtle. Sometimes abrupt, sometimes more like a leak. We need soul retrieval, recovery of the parts of us that have left. As a psychotherapist, I know how keenly our bodies and souls are connected. We are one unit. What causes illness in the psyche or disease in the body is often of spiritual origin and needs spiritual healing. Soul loss needs soul recovery.

We know that our physical health is greatly affected by our emotional and spiritual wellbeing. We know that prayer and spiritual resources aid physical recovery. So it is with psychological healing. In my work, I am constantly with people who have experienced soul loss, who feel a part of themselves is missing, who are not on their rightful path in life, who have limited energy to create an individuated self. The events in their history have to be worked through in the therapeutic process.

I am a traditional psychotherapist in many ways. I deeply believe in the healing process of the therapeutic relationship. But when I discovered shamanism, I experienced a deeper level of healing than I'd ever known for myself. Eventually, I began offering it to my clients when it was appropriate. Now, I often journey into the spirit world on behalf of people who have "lost" parts of their soul and need them retrieved in order to be well. In a soul retrieval journey, I travel with my spirit helpers to the parts of a person's soul that have been lost and bring them back for a healing.

Sometimes, it is not a therapy client but someone I've never met who is seeking shamanic healing. "I feel like something's missing," Lilly said to me on the phone.

After drumming and praying, I lay down on my mat and, close my eyes:

> I go to my spirit home and state my intention to my spirit
> guides. I immediately see an image of Lilly tied to a post. I

am reminded of someone being tortured or burned at the stake. I go on, again to waters. This time I am taken to a lovely pond where I see a young girl of about ten. She has a baby in a basket nearby. She has been taking care of the baby, sometimes letting it float gently on the waters, as if the infant is still being carried in womblike waves, an angelic amniotic sac. This is a young part of Lilly, separated from her since infancy.

When the healing is complete, I decide to mention the brief image I'd had at the beginning. Lilly smiles as she says, "Well, that is the metaphor I often use for my life!" Then I tell her about the recovery of the infant and how the energy of the little one had now been restored to her for safekeeping. It seems that Lilly had been disassociated for most of her life. Disassociation is a common state of the psyche when a part of us splits off in times of trauma. Accidents, surgeries, assaults, deaths, tragedies of many kinds create an experience so horrific for a human being, that soul loss is a beneficent salvation. Soul loss spares us. Our psyche saves us from unredeemable suffering by splitting off part of itself into the spirit world to wait until it is safe to return.

People who experience post-traumatic stress syndrome are helped as they allow buried memories to come to the surface and work through the devastating feelings they carry. But sometimes soul loss comes from more subtle, ongoing stress. It seems to be linked to the human condition. We all experience loss of soul, or soul erosion, at times. The good news is that since our soul is energy, it doesn't die. It just splits off from us, as if into some estranged energy field, but is available for return later in life.

Lilly's healing had begun when she first realized something was amiss in her unconscious. A second layer of healing, what we call "working through" in psychotherapy, is the process of dealing with the feelings that accompanied the original trauma. The third layer of healing, of paramount importance, comes when the spiritual essence which was endangered, is safely returned home to the self.

"It all started with this minister," Maryellen says with a faroff look in her eyes. Maryellen is a fiftysomething woman of Spanish descent. Her thick brunette curls suggest life and spirit. Her dark eyes usually have more fire in them. Today she is pensive, her petite body curled comfortably into a soft chair. Maryellen is telling me about an experience of many years ago. She was twenty-nine years old, had two babies at home, had a husband consumed with his work, and she was seriously depressed. This was a very dark time in her life. When she heard that her father, the closest person in the world to her, had cancer, she went to a minister for counseling. Without realizing it, she transferred her feelings for her father onto the minister, became very dependent on him and very religious. The minister's theology was based on sin and guilt so Maryellen would pray for hours about the state of her soul.

"One night as I knelt by my bed I felt my entire bedroom fill up with evil. I experienced a terror never known before or since." Maryellen's eyes grow dark and fearful. "I cried out loud, 'I call upon all the powers of heaven to come to my aid.' Gradually, the corners of the room began to fill with light. Toxicity drained out of the atmosphere and was replaced by an effervescence, as if a joyful party was in progress." Now Maryellen looks at me with the residual astonishment of that night. "I saw ten or twelve beings of light in the room, all saying to me, 'Rejoice'."

"I found my voice to say to them, 'Who are you?'"

"We're your guardian angels. We've been with you since birth."

"Their contagious joy welled up like an underground spring inside me. My depression was temporarily relieved."

Maryellen continued to see the minister. He began kissing her and holding her. She fell in love with him. She got more despondent. At the most unexpected times, like when she was vacuuming, the angels would appear, surprising her with momentary joy. In the middle of this emotional roller coaster, her father died and she felt nothing. No tears.

Maryellen decided to become a minister. She entered seminary. Then the minister, who had been counseling and fondling her, refused to see her. Confused and despairing over his rejection, Maryellen went to his office on a Saturday morning. At first, he didn't respond to her knocking, but her pleading finally brought him to the door. She went in. "Why are you treating me this way?"

"Because you are the devil incarnate," he said, a conclusion he evidently came to through his moralistic theology and his inability to control his own sexual feelings.

Maryellen believed his words. Her response was to attempt suicide. Her husband stopped her. Maryellen just said, "Help me," the last words she spoke for many days.

She was admitted to a hospital, sedated heavily, and kept in a small room where she was watched through a tiny window in the door. In a few days a young doctor came in to try to get her to eat. He said, "What is your name?"

"The Running Sewer," she replied, "The Running Sewer."

He began by feeding her soup. They began to talk. Through their work together, her will to live was restored. But at one point during her nine-month confinement, she decompensated and tried suicide again. She was put in a straight jacket.

"I felt at the bottom of the sea," Maryellen says to me. "at the lowest point on earth." Maryellen's eyes fill with tears as she remembers this terrible time in her life. She wipes her eyes and goes on. "I somehow became aware that God didn't make me in order to end up like this. I made a definite conscious decision to get well. I was determined to use every resource within me to do it. As I the angels continued to come to me. In fact, I felt so comfortable with them that I called them, 'My Gang'." Maryellen grins broadly. "They kept me company."

Although her own doctor seemed to understand and accept her visions, the head of the hospital asked her if she would meet with all the doctors and discuss her angel visitors. "I walked into a room with about a dozen men sitting in high back chairs around a large table. They bombarded me with questions. "Why do the angels come to you? Are you somebody special? How come we don't see them? Don't you know it's a figment of your imagination? Do you realize this is a part of your illness?"

"They interpreted my spiritual visions as psychoses." Maryellen sighs. "A month or so later I was called into the office of the head of the hospital. He told me that I was making progress, that they wanted me to get home, but that I couldn't be released until I stopped seeing angels."

The next time the angels came, Maryellen explained to them that in order for her to go home to her family they would have to stop coming. "I have to make it on my own now."

On the day she was to go home the Doctor asked if she still hallucinated about angels. "No, I told them to go away."

He said, "Do you admit now that you were making them up?"

"Well, I'm not sure," she replied, "but I think I have been."

Years later, Maryellen attends a workshop to learn how to do shamanic journeys. She takes to the process immediately and comes home to her soul in a joyful way. She rediscovers the angels she once renounced for sanity's sake. Maryellen recaptures her childhood wonder of nature. She begins to grow as never before, reaffirming her old pact with the Divine to use all her resources for good. She has spirit guides to help her on her path.

Maryellen becomes empowered and openhearted. Her work and her relationships are blossoming. Maryellen is incurably sane.

Marion Woodman is the Jungian analyst who has written many books on feminine psychology. She started hearing angels when she was three. Her mother thought she was crazy. When Marion was older, the angels told her about a death that would happen. When she told her mother, her mother hit Marion and told her she was to never speak of angels again. The death did occur. Marion felt sorry for her mother because of what she was missing, the angels were her life; but about the age of twelve she stopped talking about them for many years.

I do two journeys for Maryellen. The first is a soul retrieval.

I see a seven year-old on a prim and proper path away from her natural exuberance and delight in the life of spirit. This upright child masks and represses a beautiful soul. A power animal arrives to coax the girl into smiles. We invite the child to come home, telling her that grown-up Maryellen is not depressed anymore and will honor this girl's spiritual energy.

Then I'm taken to an elegant, lustrous crystal that was left behind when Maryellen entered her mother's womb. The crystal wasn't going to be safe so it remained in the spirit world. The jewel is awesome, so radiant that I cannot really see its form, only its glow.

I blow the healed seven year-old and the magnificent crystal, Maryellen's essence, into her heart and crown chakras. I speak reverently as I try to describe this journey. She incorporates the healing readily and her own journey work increases.

A few months later, Maryellen wants more healing. She's under great duress about a life decision she is making.

Four angels gather around Maryellen. They are polishing the gem that she is, the crystal brilliance of her. A fine dust had fallen around it and they remove the dust with any specks that have gotten in her way. She becomes dazzling. I don't see her body form, just this brilliance that is Maryellen. She is lustrous.

I ask for help to open up whatever path she's to choose at this time of transition. I begin to see the light shining out in front of her is spacious, as if to show many options, many possibilities. The light is strong and steady like a searchlight. It is creating a path in front of her.

I see her taking little steps, smiling and radiant. She gives me a big smile. She looks healthy, vigorous. She takes my hand. Her power animals wink at her. Each step is delicious. She follows the light almost like Dorothy followed the yellow brick road. One step leads to the next. Each brick of light brings her pleasure. She can't get lost in all this light. This is a journey of empowerment. I and my animals back away and she is on the path alone as a crystal light. HER SOUL LIGHT SHINES.

Then she comes back into her form again, with her particular body shape and life work. She takes her steps. Then she becomes the LIGHT again. Huge. Then back into her body in this world. She goes back and forth from form to essence. Beautiful to behold. She doesn't lose her pace. She just moves along. Maryellen is on her way!

I know Mary to be a survivor of incest. She grew up in a tiny town where there was no escape from her father's abuse. She has created a facade that has worked well for her and enabled her to be a successful career woman.

"I want to look good and feel good. I'm afraid of losing my sense of security if I keep telling you these things about my father." Mary's downcast body is a metaphor for the burdens she has carried all by herself for forty years. She pulls one of the pillows closer. "I want to talk about something different today."

I feel her fear and respect her need to proceed in her own way. Survivors of sexual abuse need to deal with their issues at a pace they can tolerate.

A few weeks later, Mary has a dream about adopting a puppy whom she brings to my house. She tells me, "I want you to see how well she looks and that I'm really trying to take good care of her."

Mary and I work together closely for a few years, slowly recovering the pieces of the puzzle of her childhood. Eventually, she asks for a soul retrieval.

I cannot get her to relate to me and she is also unresponsive to my power animal. We can't reach her. A deer comes into the cave. She lies beside her for a long, long time until Mary begins to notice her and trust her. The deer wins her over! Only then, is little Mary willing to leave this awful place. I tell the little girl that she's safe to come back now because Mary is grown up and will take very good care of her. I also tell her that the deer could come back with her and be her friend. Then deer and I find her lost child selves.

As I sit beside Mary and tell her what I have found, she is quiet and pensive. When I tell her about the deer, she grins and tells me about a picture of a deer which hangs over her bed. I'm not surprised.

Mary nods in understanding.

"You have the spirit of deer with you all the time. Whatever you are doing, wherever you are, whether you know it or not, this gentle creature is with you. There was a real bonding. Like a mother deer licking a newborn fawn You aren't taking care of this little girl alone anymore."

She smiles.

I go on to tell her about the work of integration. "It is important to treat yourself lovingly the next 24 hours. Be mindful of the healing that has come to you. It would be wise to spend some time with these parts that have been returned to you. Go to them. Ask them if they have something to teach you and how they can help you. They have all come back to help, to give you something. And you also need to ask them what changes you need to make to honor them and make use of the spiritual energy they are bringing to you."

"I will do that. And I'll tell you about it in our next session."

I see Mary in session only five days later. She is glowing. She reports that she can't believe how good she feels. She has put up more pictures of her new power animal and has had a remarkable sense of wellbeing as she welcomes these new parts of herself into her life.

Soul retrievals do not always have instantaneous effect. The healing may take days, weeks or months to absorb. Mary's was instantaneous and lasting. Sometimes when a soul part is returned, even though it is healed and brings helpful energy to the person, it may also bring memories and feelings which challenge the person to work with that part of herself that has been banished for so many years. In such cases, the person has the strength to be able to deal with the old traumas in a new way and the healing is also deep and lasting. Soul retrievals must be done by trained and ethical people because the experience is powerful and there may be a need for follow-up work.

Caryn begins her therapy in enormous pain. "I'm a lost cause, swimming in depression." This overwhelming feeling grows more profound as she uncovers an entire childhood of physical abuse. We travel downward through the years of terror when her father held the family hostage to his violence.

A couple of years after Caryn begins her intensive, twice a week therapy with me, I have a vision:

> I see Caryn walk towards me with her arms outstretched. I take her hands. There is a band of angels behind me and around me, as if we all together reach out toward her tears. In the far distance I see spirits behind her who are waiting and wanting to come close to surround her with their help, their sustenance.

> The more distraught she becomes in her pain, the closer her angels come, until she is sobbing into the earth and they surround her, chanting and humming their healing songs. She wails until her tears pour like a river into the earth. The louder she wails, the louder they hum. All I do is stand there with my hands stretched out towards her, as the spirits surround her.

Finally, she looks up. I put my arms around her. She's kneeling on the ground so her head rests against me about waist high, about where a child meets a mother. I hold her gently while she absorbs my spiritual presence. This takes a long time. Eventually, she backs up so my arms loosen. She looks around to see the spirits who have enveloped us.

I back away again while she apprehends the wonder of these beings of light who have come to her. At times, she speaks with them. Sometimes I listen, sometimes I guide, sometimes she does this all alone. Her bond strengthens with them and with me. She no longer kneels to wail into the earth. She begins to stand tall. I see the weight around her slowly melt away as she becomes elongated. She's still powerful in body and spirit, but more solid then soft.

Caryn stands in her circle of beings. Sometimes there are still tears and fears but when that happens, the recovery is immediate. The guidance is strong, the power does not diminish. There is much light.

I did not tell Caryn the vision at the time, but it was a sign to me of how our process would evolve. And so it did.

Caryn's father inflicted profound abuse on her and others in the family. She was devastated by the humiliating memories of his treatment of her. Eventually, her shame turns to rage.

One day, near the beginning of a session, Caryn closes her eyes and says, "I see people in white coming toward me." She shivers in fear of what's coming.

"It's okay, Caryn, tell me what you see."

"Saints and angels are gathering around me. They know I want to kill my father and they tell me it's okay. Someone puts a large sword in my hands. Someone else says, "It's a rite of passage. I'm afraid. This seems wrong."

I encourage her to let whatever wants to happen, happen. She sobs and shakes.

> They are with me. I can do this. I think of St. George slaying the dragon. I take the sword (Vehemently, she clasps something in her two hands.) and crash it down on my father's head. The sword goes through his neck, pinning him to the ground. His face is frozen. No one says anything or touches me but I know they are all around. Finally, his body shinks smaller and smaller.

Caryn comes out of her trance with a big sigh. "I feel strong and not alone. I did what I had to do." Though it has taken her years of therapy to come to this moment, once it happens she experiences a lasting relief. She has no idea of the help she will receive from the world she's just entered.

Caryn does hard work in her therapy. Dreams often guide her toward truths she needs to deal with. One day she has a dream that she is ready to dismiss. "Not much to it," she says. "I'm driving home when I notice a large tiger on the side of the road. I'm startled, especially because it's so out of place in this setting. The tiger is both fascinating and ferocious so I'm not sure what to do. I decide to get out of my car and follow him. He asks me to go to the center of the earth."

I know instinctively that the tiger is a power animal presenting himself to Caryn. Since this is not the first time the spirit world has intruded into our sessions, I sense it is appropriate for me to tell her about shamanic journeys.

Caryn is aware that she has occasionally moved into a trance-like state in sessions and that the experience is different from the regressions she also moves into. She responds with great interest when I tell her about shamanic journeys. On her first journey, Caryn finds tiger waiting for her. They walk together into his den. It is not dark but light with crystals. Gleaming walls of colored crystal shine and simmer. The tiger leads her down through the crystals to a hallway where there is an old woman who gives her the guidance she needs that day. She's found a teacher. I know she's entering a deeper level of healing.

One night, I dream about a little girl who is alone in the waiting room next to my office. She's a little blonde child of about two or three years old. I realize that she's homeless and wants to be at home with me. She stays for hours and looks at old photographs that seem to be of her mother. Caryn is somewhere in the room too.

The next day, the little girl haunts me and I decide to journey about her.

> I am taken into the upperworld. An angel appears who speaks to me. "Sharon you are on a holy task. I protect you and go with you."

> I tell her about my dream. "I'm just drawn to know more about this girl. I'm not even reading Sunday papers today. Just feel I should know more about her."

> We fly towards the land of the ancestors, a place of wisdom. Four people come and encircle me, two place their hands on my shoulders. "We know you are here for something very important."

> I tell them my dream and I say, "I want to find out who this little girl is."

> "You already know that she is Caryn."

> "Caryn. Is this the child who went into a closet to escape abuse? Why is she hanging around me?"

> The ancestor speaks again. "She's waiting to go home to Caryn. She is acting as if she is your girl but she needs to

S

come home to Caryn. You are very concerned about her, want to do what is right for this stray child, stray soul part. It's time to bring her home to herself. Right now, when Caryn leaves her session, the little girl stays."

I ask Caryn to bring in pictures of herself around the age of three. She opens an envelope, places a picture in my hand and it is nearly exactly what I saw in my dream—a cute, blonde-haired girl sitting on a wooden child's chair. I know immediately that she is waiting to be brought home to Caryn.

Caryn begins her session by telling me of her deep trust in me, her awareness that I will be here for her. In recent weeks she has been dealing with issues at the church where she has felt unappreciated and replacable, like feelings in her early childhood. Our sessions are a refuge for her.

Suddenly Caryn is overtaken by emotion and her eyes close. I know she's in another place. "Tell me what you see," I say.

> I'm about four years old, in my bed by the window. I'm looking out at the night sky. I can cry because no one hears me here. I want to melt into the wall. I want to die. I seem to disappear into the windowsill.

> Now I see a shaft of light on my bed. I don't die because the angels come. Purple and pink lights dance up and down. The angels take the grown up me to the little girl stuck in the crack of the window. The child stiffens. "Poor child," I say, "Let me hold you. You will never be alone and no one can replace you ever." The little girl blends into grown-up Caryn. Tiger stands nearby.

In the weeks following this spontaneous soul retrieval, Caryn feels terribly alone and sad, crying a lot. "I want to sleep a lot," she tells me. "I feel so broken and vulnerable. Is this how I'm supposed to feel?"

"You won't feel this way long," I say, "but this little child wants you to know her pain, how she was totally alone and at the mercy of other people's whims."

"My father did whatever he wanted to me, but my mother seems to be nowhere. I don't remember my mother's lap. I don't remember her holding me or singing to me or reading to me. I just remember, 'I'm too tired' and 'go to sleep now'. I see her back in the kitchen, in the bedroom, bent over the crib, taking care of the two younger ones."

She journeys to the little girl.

> She's wrapped in a quilt. Pain is in all the squares. "You need to feel this hurt now so you don't feel it forever," the child says. "I've come to bring you wholeness."

Another time she journeys about the child and a woman comes to speak with her.

> She's very wise and beautiful. There is a blue glow about her. I ask her about this child and she says, "What do you want to know?"

> "What happened to this child?"

> "What happens to many children. They get lost, destroyed."

> "What am I supposed to remember?"

> "The sadness, the sacredness. Remember the grief." Caryn is shown other children who are lost. "Know that there's vulnerability in everyone, so that you may have compassion. And know that you are never alone, that you have me and tiger and the others."

The accumulation of these spiritual experiences, which seem exquisitely timed to fit into her process in psychotherapy, bring substantial change in Caryn. Just as her psyche always seems to know just when she is ready to uncover a new memory from her past, and would somehow be able to deal with it, so her own psyche\soul seems to know just when she's ready for a spiritual healing that she will be able to integrate. I trust the process in her completely and am guided by a Wisdom greater than my own. Internally, she lived precariously close to the edge of a black hole which could have swallowed her; but her capacity to use spiritual resources has not only guaranteed her survival but also turned her toward a productive life.

Caryn's need for shamanic healing tends to arrive in the middle of her therapy sessions. One day she's telling me about a dream in which she needs surgery in her liver area. She sees an outline of a kidney shaped tumor that has risen to the surface of her skin and is ready to come out. After she tells me about it, she looks at me and says, "I don't think I can do this. Can you?"

I know she needs an extraction, a journey into the spirit world to remove the toxic energy that is implanted in her. Extractions are somewhat opposite to soul retrievals. In soul retrievals we return spiritual energy to the soul. In extractions, we remove energy that has been intrusive and causes illness of some sort or another. This traditional shamanic practice is to extract the spiritual component to a physical or emotional disease. I get out my drum and incense.

> I journey to the spirits who show me a solid mass on her right side. As I rise up to do the healing, I notice that her saints and angels form a circle around us. They are here to help.

> I work slowly to gradually loosen the tumor underneath and then I remove it.

> Then I'm shown that her golden heart is encased in a black tire-shaped mass. We are to pull this out also. This mass

shielding her heart is stubborn. One of her angels hands me
a feather, which helps cut away the tire. It comes out in bits
and pieces. Then I pat light into the area. One by one her
spirits come and place their hands above the two areas of
extraction, offering their blessing.

Caryn says she saw feathers and fur during the extraction, and
felt lightness and contentment. She immediately feels better. She
has a dream which leads her to say, "The most important thing in
the world is my relationship to God."

Healing is a spiritual affair. Whether disease begins in the body
and impacts the soul, or the reverse, it always can be helped by the
spirit world. To lose one's soul is the gravest occurrence of all, since
it would eliminate any meaning from life

Barbara Brennan teaches about the painful feeling of being
torn apart when a loved one is lost in divorce or death or
abandonment. When the relational cords are damaged, people are
left disillusioned, bewildered, and in havoc. She points out that in
any separation, certain cords must dissolve, but others remain.
When two people have loved each other, the cords that represent
the love remain through the transition, while the unhealthy cords
are severed and healed.

Bonds continue, where there has been true love, and we do
ourselves a great disservice by demeaning former love choices or
dishonoring people with whom we spent significant energy.

One soul retrieval for a woman who had finally ended an abusive
marriage, brought her great healing:

I see a skeleton, the part of her that wasted away in forty
years of marriage. We go to the desert where I often find
healing. Angels blow life into this skeleton. One angel gives
her a key, the key to her new life.

After blowing this healing into this woman, I see an immediate joy flush her face. In following months as she returns for heal-

ing work, her serious health worries subside, her emotions stabilize, and she is literally radiant. Even people at her place of work notice the difference.

If our loved ones are not able to do sacred closure with us, we can still do the work in our own souls. We can go into the spirit world for a ritual. I once journeyed for someone whose husband had died suddenly. Louise had been in acute grief for too long.

> I'm told to take out the bones in her that are knit to her husband. I see a left rib coming out. "The same for him," I hear. A right rib somehow comes from him. We put them in the fire.

> "She not willing to do anymore grieving," I say.

> "No, she doesn't need to." The ashes are gathered together and placed in a white container. I hear the words, "The ashes are forever mixed. Honor what has been."

Relationships can be deepened even after death if the departed one has gone on to the light and is available in a helpful way.

Molly is attending my introductory workshop to learn how to do shamanic journeys. On her very first journey she is stunned to meet her father who had died when she was eight.

As she sits up to write down what she has experienced, Molly's eyes fill with tears and she becomes silent, holding to herself the immense emotion of the reunion. Then she puts down her journal to speak about her journey. She tells about how he just appeared to her and then she begins to remember the night of his death in vivid detail—the phone call, her mother's hysteria, her task of comforting her younger sister and keeping them both "out of the way".

"I have been grieving for him for nearly thirty years," she says. "But I never felt it." Her wet cheeks glisten as she tells us about how this man who died had been her love, a daddy who doted on her in many ways. "I used to wait in the window for him to come home from work. And on weekends he would take me out for ice cream."

Molly needed to split off from the trauma of that death, almost banishing that part of herself that couldn't cope with the tragedy. At first she had buried her feelings because she needed to help take care of her sister and then she soon felt the need to accommodate her mother's inconsolable lament. As she got out of touch with her own grief, she became invested in not knowing her feelings because they were too hard to bear. Now a gradual healing is in effect. She is retrieving the part of herself that had frozen in grief at the time of her father's sudden death. Interestingly, she becomes cold whenever she talks about this subject in the weeks to come.

She decides to do a journey with me present as a guide. Her intention is to go to the time in childhood that would help her thaw and heal:

> I hear somebody crying, very far away. Heart-wrenching sobs. Now I see the little girl. She's very scared, all alone, and her fists are clenched in anger. No one is paying attention to her. "I just have to take care of myself," she says.

> I walk up to her and slowly take her hand. The girl is so sad it breaks my heart. I walk past scenes in her life—see her running to the door to greet her father, sitting in a room with her brother, praying for a sister, sleeping in her parents' bed after her father left for work.

> Then my power animal comes up to the little girl and she pets him. This makes her happy and she even smiles.

> Suddenly my father appears and stands between me and the little girl. He's blocking my view of the child. "I didn't want to leave you," he says. "I'm sorry it hurt so much."

> I'm very angry with him and tell him so. He moves aside. I
> go over to the little girl and lift her into my heart.

Molly has retrieved part of her soul. She is puzzled at her anger at her father, but also feels he has been "in her way", keeping the hurt child hidden behind him so that Molly didn't see her need for comfort. Now that she has freed the child from hiding behind her father's back by telling her father to move aside, Molly is able to pay attention to the child's needs and get on with her life.

"I saw an angel come to you when your father moved aside," I say. "I think you've been given help."

A few months later, Molly journeys again.

> I see three angels surrounding me in a field. They open a
> path for my father who walks in. "You left," I say to him.
>
> "But you can talk with me anytime you surround yourself
> with these angels."

Molly's profound feelings of abandonment begin to heal as these journeys give her the reunion with her father and the freedom from him she has always needed. In a paradoxical way, she now has more of him and she is also free of him.

Death loses its power as we travel deeply into spirit. Our relationships do not die because a person does. We need to maintain the health of the bond between ourselves and others, so that when death comes, we are not left with unresolved feelings. Or soul loss. If relationships are contaminated in life, we are left with much to cleanse. If our cords are clean, we will have a purer mourning. I am taught this on a journey:

> My teacher looks into my eyes. "In the future, you must
> keep all cords clear in important relationships. Let nothing
> toxic accumulate; do not be in any relationship that is toxic.

"I understand. Will you help me?"

"You have a lot to learn about this. We will help you. You are going to become sensitized so that if something abusive is coming towards you, you will deter it. It will be like a tinkling bell sings inside you to turn you from harm towards goodness."

I smile at her. She puts her left arm around me. She leads me as if I am blind, slowly around the circle four times. She stops. Asks me to look into the fire. We do a ritual.

Bringing the soul home from death can also be from our own death, or dismemberment. Kelly is a therapist and a natural caretaker; today she wants help knowing how to limit her level of involvement with others so as not to wear herself out. A common issue for women!

I see Kelly lying on a small grassy hillside in a meadow. Light beams down on her and then becomes fiercely penetrating. The heat scorches her, begins to burn away her skin, cells, muscle and tissue till only her bones are left. The bones are parched white in the light. Then they, too, dissolve into dust. There is no Kelly left.

A soft bluish white light appears in a gentle swirl. The light creates a small whirlwind where Kelly had been, then either creates or gathers tiny particles that flurry into the form of Kelly. Suddenly she is encased in an egg of lovely light and she is radiant. Her whole self is a beaming smile.

"Tell Kelly to call Spirit," I'm told as the journey ends.

As I tell Kelly about the dismemberment journey I just had for her, I am struck by an association to Ezekiel. Remember how God led Ezekiel to the valley of dry bones? The Holy Voice speaks to Ezekiel and says, "O dry bones, hear the word of the Lord . . .

Behold, I will cause breath to enter you, and you shall live." The bones start rattling and come together, sinew and flesh come to cover them. The Voice also says, "I will put my Spirit within you and you shall live."

A classical experience in shamanism is the dismemberment journey, which occurs as a person is being initiated further along the path. Sometimes, whether in Samiland or in a suburban living room, a person will experience a dismemberment, which is a healing of transfomation. It always includes re-memberment, a putting the bones back together in a new way. It is a breaking up of the old you, a reduction to dust or nothing at all, as in a death, and then a rebirth.

So much dying has to happen for us to live more fully. Not a new spiritual teaching, is it? I think of the great shaman, Jesus, who brought back people from death, whose healing and teaching often was about our need to die in order to be born.

Sometimes it's not a person who has died but a whole way of life. One woman, a healer herself, comes regularly for her own treatment while she is going through one devastation after another. Her life is not like Job's but it does render her victim of circumstances beyond her control. And yes, she works on issues of control, trying to let go and grow in soul while everything falls apart around her. One day when I journey for her, I am led back to a verse in Scripture that I haven't read in many years. "Beloved, do not be surprised at the fiery ordeal which comes upon you to prove you, as though something strange were happening to you . . ." and goes on to describe the spiritual battle and victory that can be hers if she endures. These words bring immediate recognition and joy to her. "Yes, I know that's what's going on." And she takes heart. Or is given heart.

More and more, Jesus, scripture and old Christian traditions find their place in my healing work, jumping out with clarity and power I never knew before. I am grateful. Sometimes, I'm moved and shaken beyond words.

I don't meant to imply that shamanic healing operates like a magic wand, though often an immediate effect is felt. But even if the spiritual healing takes time to assimilate and integrate, it can be a profound adjunct to the work of psychotherapy.

One time I did a soul retrieval for someone and found her at twenty-two, seated in a dark room with an angel behind her. This young woman had been through terror but the guardian was keeping watching all these years. "Yes," my client said. "I was nearly killed in a car accident at that time."

"One of the times I really didn't listen to my feelings was when I had my abortion," Andrea says sadly, her eyes welling with tears. "I still have guilt about that experience." Finally she feels safe to tell me about it. She goes on to talk about it and, as our session ends, she asks if she could have a soul retrieval. We do that the next session.

> I'm taken to several parts of young Andrea and then I see, or perhaps it's more accurate to say, I sense a tiny aborted spirit, a blob of being. An angel picks it up lovingly. She speaks, and gives Andrea a rose. She says Andrea should get herself one as a reminder to thank this little one for being with her a short time. She also needs to thank herself for giving the being a home for the brief span it took for the spirit to know this was not the right time to come.

Since that day, Andrea has kept a rose in her kitchen, which brings her joy. She has let go of her guilt and embraced that early pregnancy in a new way. She has also become conversant with the angel.

I don't know if beings choose wombs where they'll be aborted, if they and the soul of the parents need that experience for their growth. I don't know any more than anyone does about the soul of the being in the womb; but I report honestly what is shown me on journeys.

I'm remembering a woman who came for a soul retrieval who

had had many devastating deaths in her life. She was only in her forties and had lost many of the key people in her life. The healing in her soul retrieval was about finding her original soul's blessing.

> I'm taken up into an ethereal place of stars and glimmer. Dazzling. I see my client dressing for a date, perhaps a prom. She's wearing a lovely white dress with a net skirt.

> An angel arrives and gives me a magic wand to bless her; as the wand touches her, she is filled with love and abundance. Feeling like a fairy godmother with Cinderella, I watch her become glittering light and I hear a voice, "Her date is life."

Our truest self is restored in soul retrievals, sometimes including our very purpose in being here. Our date IS life, the magic of living in the Light from which we came and to which we go.

Luminous Journeys

We have been journeying to the spirit world through natural portals. In this section of the book, *Luminous Journeys* uses photographs from nature as doorways to divination. These doors welcome you to truths to help you with your life. As you work with the images, you will find them portals into illumination. Also, you will find that you begin seeing these portals yourself more and more out in nature as Spirit calls to you.

You are invited to the guidance of Spirit. You are encouraged to listen for the voice within. Synchronicity of icon and imagination will dance together. Let the next pages of this journal choose you, as if they were cards to be shuffled and then one drawn.

Since ancient times, symbols and images have been used for divination. Petroglyphs, tree lines, runes, tarot cards, and other gateways to knowing have been a part of human history. Those who develop their intuition become very gifted in reading the signs before them.

When you are ready to proceed, sit quietly and invite your spirit guides to be present. Later, if you have trouble understanding an image, you can look to your guide for assistance. Become clear about your intention, what specific issue you would like to bring to the oracles. Become as succinct as possible about the issue before you. The more specific your intention, the more helpful will be the message back to you. Do not register this as a yes or no question. Rather, a request for guidance and illumination. Examples are: "I need clarity on how to handle the negativity I'm feeling toward my boss at work." "I'm struggling with whether to follow my interest in photography." "I need guidance of my tendency to sabotage my healing of addiction. . . ." "What can I most offer my child at this time?"

Next, close your eyes. While stating your intention, shuffle through the next pages and let your fingers find which one wants to speak to your issue. Or, close the book, state your intention and then blindly to one of these last pages knowing it is your helper for today.

This image will speak to your situation. Gaze into the picture and let a stream of consciousness come to you. What does the image suggest to you? What flows to you? After your own musings, let the words by the picture engage you yet more deeply. On each page, "For Reflection" suggests three additional ways to further integrate the wisdom the portal is bringing to you.

The first times you land on a page, you can write in this journal. In future times, you can keep accompanying journals as you can draw the same page many times in life. Just like tarot cards or runes. Let the images become your friends over the years.

Sometimes the images will be so obvious to you that you will say, "I already know that." And you can be grateful for the validation. Other times you will feel frustrated. "I don't want to hear that. I'm tired of this." Let the image be a support to you, even though it's not the news you wanted. Sometimes you will feel joy or excitement. Or renewed commitment. Or conviction about right action.

You can use this process any day or every day, by yourself in solitary meditation or in a circle with others. You can do this with a partner and give each other associations and feedback. You can do the work in a small group where you take turns and support each other in sacred circle. You could also hold the image in your head and journey with an intention slightly different than the one suggested on the page. Journey through it with your power animal on an intention relevant to your issue. You will find your own creative ways. Maybe they will inspire a poem or a painting. Let them be a bridge to your higher self, an access to the spirit world where all your needs are met. May you find portals everywhere.

SHARON BLESSUM

# 1. Opening

Even in what seems frozen, an opening appears to invite you into a new place. Look carefully and you will see the issue before you as an opportunity that has been hidden. In fact, stark beauty surrounds the entrance to a new world. Light gleams off the portal. You may need to shapeshift, to rearrange your ideas, preconceptions, beliefs, in order to fit into this new possibility—but you will be glad you did.

*For Reflection:*
1. Journey into the spirit world and ask for help to locate the opening before you that you might find the surprising possibility in this issue.
2. Journey through the opening in this image to receive a song, affirmation, body movement, prayer, ritual, or gift.
3. What action will you take to honor the guidance of this opening?

be
Thou
my vision

# 2. Vision

This is a time of blurred sight. You are not clear about where you are going or what you are doing. Now is a wondrous opportunity to entrust your life to the Great Thou. The old hymn sings, "Be Thou my wisdom, and Thou my true word . . . Heart of my own heart, whatever befall . . . Thou be my vision. . . ." Relief comes when you know you are not alone, that everywhere you are, God is. Let the great Source of All take charge of your life and your path will become clear.

*For Reflection:*
1. You might like to read Psalm 139, or some other sacred scripture that links you to the Holy Presence that is in every part of you and your life.
2. Journey into this path, asking Spirit for a song, affirmation, body movement, prayer, ritual, or gift.
3. What action will you take to honor the guidance of this image?

O Great Light
beyond
the shadows,
lead me
home.

SHARON BLESSUM

# 3. Night Medicine

In the great night of the soul, in the deep midnight of every day, in the tunnel of a long passage, Light appears to call us and remind us of our true home. Whatever shadows seem to be haunting you, let them be as beauty to frame the moonmedicine that passes through all nights with you. Let there be Light . . . .

*For Reflection:*
1.  Journey to your spirit guide and ask to be taken to the magic and mystery of night medicine.
2.  Meet the spirit of moon to receive a song, affirmation, body movement, prayer, ritual, or gift.
3.  What action will you take to honor the guidance of this image?

SHARON BLESSUM

# 4. Mystery

Now is the time to leave your fears on the shore. Walk the dock into the Great Mystery. Walk on the waters. Head to another shore. Swim. Surrender. Glide. You will be carried to the horizon of Light. The serenity of that distant land will meet you. Mystery invites the fall into freedom.

*For Reflection:*
1. Journey into the scene for further illumination.
2. Dive into the portal of this image to receive a song, affirmation, body movement, prayer, ritual, or gift.
3. What action will you take to honor the guidance of this image?

Cathedrals
hold the prayers
of the ancient ones

SHARON BLESSUM

# 5. Ancient Prayers

Do you know that you are prayed for? That others, known and unknown, hold you in healing Light? The very rocks chant beauty and supplication on your behalf. All creation is singing to each other. Awareness of eternal prayers will change your life. Prayers of the old ones still reverberate in timeless waves of energy on your behalf. Your prayers for future generations will land in rocks and ripples also.

*For Reflection:*
1. Journey to the red rocks, to a circle of ancient ones who are at prayer.
2. Walk into the sacred landscape of this image to receive a song, body movement, affirmation, prayer, ritual or gift.
3. What action will you take to honor the guidance of these rocks?

don't
fence
me
out

SHARON BLESSUM

# 6. Fence

Oh, we human beings are so good at blocking the light ourselves, and then wondering why it is kind of dark. You need not peer through a fence. You can open the gate, take down the barricade, demolish the barrier that has been created between you and Spirit, you and Light, you and another, you and abundance. Perhaps you built the wall out of de-fences needed from earlier years. You may not even know you did it. But now is the time to let in what's on the other side!

*For Reflection:*
1. Ask your spirit guides to lovingly show you what fences you have created that keep others away from you, keep joy away from you, keep Light away from you. Then, ask them to help you take them down.
2. Journey into this image to receive a song, affirmation, body movement, prayer, ritual, or gift.
3. What action will you take to honor the guidance of this image?

SHARON BLESSUM

# 7. Earthcaves

The Greatmother has dark spaces, holy places, where you can curl into her body and rest. She is beckoning you into her secret chambers. The time for nourishment is near. Climb the steps into Her cave. You are invited to hibernate. Whatever the season of the year, you need to quiet yourself in a temporary retreat. Give yourself some seclusion, wrap yourself in the loveliness of nature, and settle into a warm, dark space where you can nurture yourself. Take time to sort things out, do not rush into activity. This is not a time for motion but for meditation. Welcome the period of quiet as a corrective to a pace that has distracted you from your soul.

*For Reflection:*
1. Journey into an earthcave to lean into the body of the Greatmother.
2. Enter the cave of this image to receive a song, affirmation, body movement, prayer, ritual or gift.
3. What action will you take to honor the guidance of this nurture?

SHARON BLESSUM

# 8. Passage

Veer your life into the beckoning beauty. Steer away from the crowds, noise, and clatter. You are ready to pass into uncharted waters. Let yourself be surprised. Spirit has a better idea! There is more stored up for you than you would know how to imagine on your own; but you must be willing to direct your voyage into territory that will be new and novel. Take a deep breath and go for it!

*For Reflection:*
1. Ask Spirit to show you where to find the portal that will allow you to move off into a new landscape.
2. Sail through this passage to receive a song, affirmation, body movement, prayer, ritual, or gift.
3. What action will you take to honor the guidance of this image?

Sharon Blessum

# 9. The Mask

Now is the time to shed your mask. You have learned well how to cover up who you really are. You know how to hide your real feelings. You have been afraid to show your truth. Let your mask crumble away. Take the risk of being your most authentic self. As the protective covering falls away, we are opened, exposed in new ways. We need to honor this transition, that new strength can emerge. Strength is borne of vulnerability. Healing and love await you.

*For Reflection:*
1. Journey to a spirit guide who will teach you how you developed a false self and have now outgrown your need for a mask. Ask the guide to show you how to safely be yourself in the world.
2. Wear the mask in this image to receive a hidden song, affirmation, body movement, prayer, ritual, or gift.
3. What action will you take to honor the guidance of this image?

mirror, mirror
on the lake
who is...

SHARON BLESSUM

# 10. Mirrors

It is time to take a good look at yourself. Maybe you need to see your beauty as never before. Maybe you need to identify some flaws you've been deftly avoiding. You are ready for more truth about yourself. You may find surprising reflections. Things are not always as they seem. Much is illusion. Peer deeper to find the truth shining in the depths, calling to you, remembering that all that has been created is good. How are you doing with the creation of you?

*For Reflection:*
1. Ask the waters to still, that you might truly see yourself as you are. Invite your spirit guides and maybe your sacred circle of friends, to help you see your truths in a loving way.
2. Leap into the mirroring waters and ask to receive a song, affirmation, body movement, prayer, ritual, or gift.
3. What action will you take to honor the guidance of these waters?

lift into the lightness
of your being

SHARON BLESSUM

# 11. Lightness of Being

Raise your eyes into the skies for illumination. Look up from your daily rounds. You are being pulled down by everyday concerns that don't really deserve this much of your life's energy. Please, dear human being, go outside and ask the sky for messages. Or close your eyes and fly into the upper realms. You are not just dense matter but also a being of light.

*For Reflection:*
1.  Journey to a spirit in the upper world who will heal and lighten you.
2.  Lift through into this portal to receive a song, affirmation, body movement, prayer, ritual or gift.
3.  What action will you take to honor the guidance of this image?

our lives emerge
from the mist
dancing

Sharon Blessum

# 12. Dancing Lives

Do you see the dance of trees? The choreography of clouds? The yoga pose of rocks? Your limbs are being called to sway, strut, and stretch to the music of the universe. Maybe you need to put on your favorite music and dance. Maybe you need to lie still with soft music and let the vibrations heal your body. It is time to emerge from the cocoon, the cave, the quiet. Let the dance begin.

*For Reflection:*
1. Journey to the music that Spirit wants you to hear, which might be in trees, caves, water, or wind. Dance with your power animal.
2. Step into the swing of the trees and let them give you a song, affirmation, body movement, prayer, ritual or gift.
3. What action will you take to honor the guidance of this image?

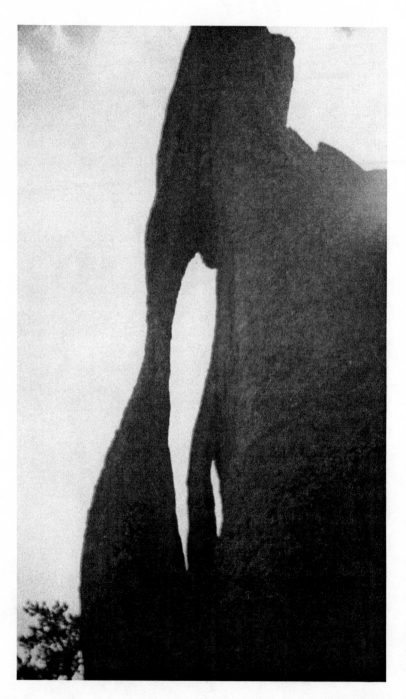

SHARON BLESSUM

# 13. Needle's Eye

Through the needle's eye, threads unseen sew two worlds together. Sometimes the veil between the worlds seems thin as lace; sometimes it seems thick as rock. Even hard rocks can connect you to the eternal, that which is durable. You need the Infinite at this time. Know that you are not just floating through this experience but that there are rocks to listen to, hide in, stand on, lean into, as you find your way. Invite a rock to open as a portal for you.

*For Reflection:*
1. Journey to the spirit of this rock for messages to help you.
2. Leap through the needle's eye and find a song, affirmation, body movement, prayer, ritual or gift.
3. What action will you take to honor the guidance of this image?

follow the path
toward your vision

SHARON BLESSUM

# 14. The Road Taken

You are ready to move on from the crossroads and turn off on your own route. "I took the one less traveled by, and that has made all the difference," Frost wrote. Yes, you are strong enough to do that also. You are ready to make a choice that is very important, if not popular to others. Do not be swayed by the need to please others, to look back, to weigh all sides. You've done that; it's time to follow your vision.

*For Reflection:*
1. Journey to your spirit guides to ask for clarity and courage to follow your vision.
2. Walk down this road to receive a song, affirmation, body movement, prayer, ritual, or gift.
3. What action will you take to honor the guidance of this image?

SHARON BLESSUM

# 15. Old Hag

Her face emerges with reassuring wisdom and strength. In the midst of the fields of life, She offers Herself. But Her presence comes with a cost. You must be willing to live deeply to even see Her; you must be willing to live authentically to be seen by Her. She is obscured through centuries of repression and denigration, but She has not disappeared. She is returning in full power to those who will open their eyes and heart to Her magic.

*For Reflection:*
1. You are ready to turn from familiar concepts of the old woman toward power of the true feminine. Journey to the Old Hag's wisdom.
2. Step into Her presence to receive a song, affirmation, body movement, prayer, ritual, or gift.
3. What action will you take to honor the guidance of this image?

SHARON BLESSUM

# 16. Lifelines

The lines of your life narrate where you have been, as may the wrinkles of your face! Each line is treasured history. If you follow the intricate path, you will find inroads to the core of you. Let the wonder of your own life become real to you. Be astonished at the pattern that is being laid down. Be aware of how important your choices are. The tracks you make today make up the footprints of your life. Today's decisions effect the rest of your lifelines forever. Choose carefully.

*For Reflection:*
1. Look at yourself in the mirror and then look at your life in the mirror. Study the lifelines and then follow them to your core to have better insight on choices before you.
2. Follow the lifelines into the treetrunk to receive a song, affirmation, body movement, prayer, ritual, or gift.
3. What action will you take to honor the guidance of this image?

SHARON BLESSUM

# 17. The Old Ones

You are ready to be taught new medicine by the Old Ones. The invisible ones who walked before you have love and lessons yet to share. Their medicine, their craft, their wise ways, are a resource to us in our lives. The Old Ones watch for those who want to learn the old ways and use them as healing help in our lives. Invite any ancestors into your lives who would be there for your highest good and truly help your life.

*For Reflection:*
1. Journey to an ancestor who wants to teach you his/her ways that could be good medicine for the ills of your life.
2. Enter this parade of stone people to receive a song, affirmation, body movement, prayer, ritual, or gift.
3. What action will you take to honor the guidance of this image?

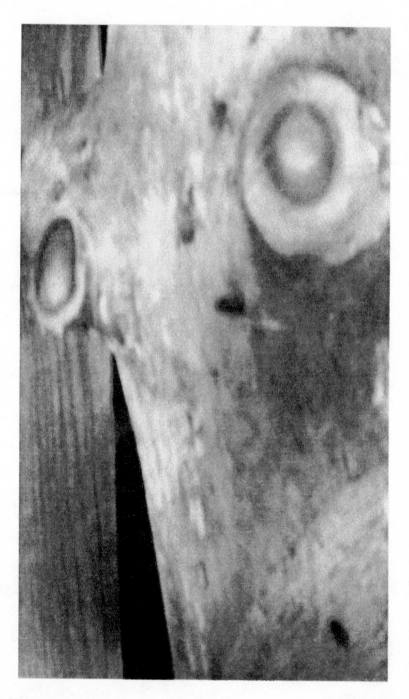

SHARON BLESSUM

# 18. Nourishment

The Greatmother offers Herself in many forms. She came as Mary, mother to a great shaman and mothering to us. Her abundance appears here in tree form; she is also seen in caves, clouds, flower and water. In Her loving gaze is the knowing we need in this lifetime. In Her compassionate heart is the embrace that holds our childlike needs. She is available to nurture you, to give you Her holy milk as you bring your thirsty soul to the motherenergy of Spirit.

*For Reflection:*
1. Your needs for mothering right now can be met in the spirit world. Ask your helpers in the upper realms to take you to motherenergy.
2. Drink from this image and receive a song, affirmation, body movement, prayer, ritual, or gift.
3. What action will you take to honor the guidance of this feminine energy?

s

Earth, fire, water and air
say goodnight
in benedictive light.

Sharon Blessum

# 19. Evening

Evening has come and you are called to the cycles of nature to guide you through the ending of this issue before you. Maybe you protest the dying of the light, rage or resent or have remorse over the day now spent. Here is your opportunity to look over the past with gratitude for what was good, healing for what was wounded, and learning for what lessons came. Receive the benediction of this faithful evening ritual.

*For Reflection:*
1. Journey to a spirit guide who will help you with the evening energy that you are in. Ask for healing to end this day with peace in your heart.

2. Rest in this portal and receive a song, affirmation, body movement, prayer, ritual, or gift.

3. What action will you take to honor the guidance of this image?

fall
in love
with God

be
willing
to be
broken

answer
the
call

be initiated
enter the sacred landscape
pass through the narrow
give up all that you have

# 20. The Call

Much of life is spent developing your particular skills, educating your mind, creating relationships, healing from childhood wounds, grieving losses, discovering your likes and dislikes, recovering from poor choices, exploring the world, etc. The first decades of life are important groundwork for the time when it is all put up for question as you are faced with the true meaning of your life. You are now being asked to leap into the deepest yes you can give, to listen to you inner voice, to follow your heart's passion, to serve Spirit.

*For Reflection:*
1. The truth of your high calling is within you. Journey to a spirit guide for illumination on the unique course you are to follow at this time.
2. Pass through this image to receive a song, affirmation, body movement, prayer, ritual, or gift.
3. What action will you take to honor the guidance of this invitation?

*YOU*

You

are a natural portal

to the spirit world.

You are a portal

for Spirit

into the natural world.


You are a threshold.

You are a gateway.

You are an opening.

You are luminous.